T0300123

The Market

This punchy book unites mainline mathematical economics and sometimes idiosyncratic political economy. Freshness is brought to the market concept giving general equilibrium theory a new lease of life, and an opening of thought on such matters as free trade, globalization and the environment.

Where most theories of general equilibrium have been based on utility maximizing traders, Afriat here maintains the view that the topic essentially is concerned with aggregates and that anything to do with utility is at best secondary if not spurious. The book goes on to discuss political economy, in particular the idea of 'optimum', and its abuses, especially in doctrine related to the market.

This novel book will be of equal appeal to mathematical thinkers, those interested in the theory of markets and political economists.

S. N. Afriat, currently associated with the University of Siena, Italy, has a long and distinguished record of publishing at the interface of mathematics and economics.

Routledge Frontiers of Political Economy

The Market

equilibrium, stability, mythology

S. N. Afriat

Routledge
Taylor & Francis Group

LONDON AND NEW YORK

First published 2003
by Routledge
2 Park Square, Milton Park, Abingdon, Oxon, OX14 4RN

Simultaneously published in the USA and Canada
by Routledge
711 Third Avenue, New York, NY 10017

Routledge is an imprint of the Taylor & Francis Group, an informa business

Typeset in 10/12 pt Times New Roman by
Newgen Imaging Systems (P) Ltd, Chennai, India

British Library Cataloguing in Publication Data
A catalogue record for this book is available
from the British Library

Library of Congress Cataloging in Publication Data
A catalog record for this book has been requested

ISBN 978-0-415-30048-3

For Benjamin Higgins
a decade later

Contents

Foreword

This short book is a heady mixture of mainstream formal mathematical economics and sometimes idiosyncratic political economy. The formal mathematical economics contains entirely original approaches to some old problems, expressed in a fresh way. The informal political economy opens valuable new avenues for thought on such matters as free-trade, globalization and the environment. One may well disagree with the latter, but the nature of political economy is that it is controversial. Even where one disagrees most vigorously one can well feel enriched by having to take on board what this most readable writer has set out.

The formal mathematical economics (my own main interest) concerns the heart of the matter – general equilibrium theory. This is a subject often, albeit mistakenly, perceived as being sterile. It is, however, refreshingly brought to, or rather given a new lease of, life in this book. The author takes pains to motivate the discussion; he introduces and uses some novel mathematics in dealing with it; and manages to combine the static and dynamic elements of the subject in an integrated treatment of existence and stability.

The material throughout is highly innovative, but more in dealing with some old, and central, problems in a new way rather than addressing the most fashionable problems of the day. Although the author is essentially an economist's economist, this book will appeal to many working in mathematics, philosophy and political theory – though only those at the more formal end of things. The stall which he sets out in this book will not appeal to everyone, but to those to whom it does appeal, it will appeal immensely.

Michael Allingham
Magdalen College, Oxford

Preface

This book is made up of several more or less self-contained parts. The material is largely unpublished, and any that is related to some form of publication before would usually have elements originating in my 1987 book *Logic of Choice and Economic Theory*.

Where the work concerns the subject of General Equilibrium, treated in Parts I, II and III, it has three main aspects. First is the motivation, and the consideration of what that subject really is about. Some would take it that everything here is well understood by everyone so there is no need for a comment and one can pass quickly to the mathematics. Here, nonetheless, a definite pause is made before that passage. That leads to the second main aspect, the mathematical. Here there are essential differences from other treatments, in terms of hypotheses, and conclusions, and methods of arriving at them.

The treatment of general equilibrium[1] maintains the view, held clearly by Schumpeter but without much comment elsewhere, that the topic has essentially to do with aggregates, and any modelling of underlying elements, in particular anything to do with utility, is secondary if not spurious. Most theories of general equilibrium have been based on utility maximizing traders. Whether or not there should be a complaint exactly here, there can be one of another order about the 'welfare' appendages to such theory.

But still, making the market, as usual, a simple sum of completely separate individual optimizing consumers and producers, besides for whatever it may be worth for purposes of illustration, has another seemingly generally unnoticed merit. This is where, according to our observation, it provides a setting for a resolution of the age-old value-problem of Aristotle.[2]

Part III on "The Linear Market Model" continues with the mathematical work within the framework laid out in Part II. Instead of being in some way advanced, it is a rewarding step towards the elementary, and to a highly instructive and interesting

---

1 In some part coming from my *Logic of Choice and Economic Theory*, Oxford: Clarendon Press, 1987, and the more recent *Quaderno* No. 264 (September 1999), "Market Equilibrium and Stability", Department of Political Economy, University of Siena.
2 See Note 1 on "Aristotle's Value Problem and General Equilibrium".

special case[3] which, in its own good way, has the important features of the general case but admits treatment by finite algebra, shown here in the Appendix and in any case already familiar from the theory of Markov processes.

For the more mathematical Parts II and III, for the purpose of making them self-contained and not overcrowded, auxiliary mathematics is supplied in an appendix. This may be already well known from other connections, or entirely peculiar to this work, as in the case of Appendix III in, Part II, which serves for the approach to stability theory.

The "Market & Myth" of Part IV is representative of the third main aspect of the work, on the side of political economy, and having concern with the idea of an "optimum," and its abuses, especially in doctrine related to the market.[4] Here is a hazardous disregard for Karl Popper's "anti-essentialist exhortation",[5] where he deals with "the principle of never arguing about words and their meanings".

The essay "On Trade, and Self-sufficiency," in Part V, based in large part on the earlier versions of 1988 in Japan and 1989 in Australia[6] and on my 1989 book, was prepared for the 1991 "Symposium on Equity and Efficiency in Economic Development in Honour of Benjamin Higgins" but as a result of McGill/Queens- related accidents became put aside. Returning to it in February 1997, I have been much indebted to Ginette Benoit, of the Canadian Institute for Research on Regional Development, Moncton NB, for her editing which came only then to my attention. Besides acceptance of almost all her suggestions, other changes include references to the Symposium volume of 1993[7] and later items. Now in year 2002 returning to it again, it begins to appear dated, as may be due in part to happenings in the meanwhile. Also the "Crisis in Economic Theory" which had been a lively subject seems now to have been successfully forgotten. Despite such obsolescence, commentary made on that subject has been retained. For the rest–perhaps it still belongs to the future!

For a defect – with a message – the book may be remarked to fall into two parts that have nothing to do with each other. A reader has identified the parts very well as "formal mathematical economics" (FME), and ["sometimes"] "idiosyncratic

---

3 Also Curtis Eaves, Operations Research Department, Stanford, has a linear model, but different, as came out of my talk on "The Linear Market" given to his Department, 23 April 1987. Though *merely* the linear case" for some reader, it can still be rated a discovery of good quality, a fresh touch for a tired subject.

4 Originally prepared at Bilkent University, Ankara, and presented at the Bosphorus Workshop on Economic Design XV, from Marmaris on the Aegean, 29 August to 5 September 1992. A later version was presented at the 2nd International Conference, The Society for Social Choice and Welfare, University of Rochester, New York, July 8–11, 1994.

5 Touched on in his *Unended Quest: An Intellectual Autobiography*, Routledge 1992 edition, Sections 6–7.

6 I acknowledge with thanks my debt to Jim Alvey, of Macquarie University, NSW, for drawing my attention to the article of J. M. Keynes of 1933 on "National self-sufficiency".

7 Irving Brecher and Donald J. Savoie (Eds), *Equity and Efficiency in Economic Development: Symposium in honour of Benjamin Higgins*. Montreal: McGill-Queen's University Press, 1993.

political economy" (IPE).[8] This book supports that FME contributes nothing to IPE. The parts are joined, and come together in the volume, simply from both being topics to do with the market.

A related complaint is that, in service as a treatise on general equilibrium, there is neglect of the important topic of optimality. True, that topic is not in the FME part. However, a dedication to its deflation can be observed in the IPE part. Reminded of it, I added a note on "The First and Second Theorems of Welfare Economics," those great hymns of market philosophy, with a treatment somewhat different from the usual.

An expansion of declared regret is that the book gets no further than the Arrow-Debreu model, despite a distinct contribution of the book being a fresh start for the well-worn topic which involves not dealing with that model at all.

The first chapter is an exploration of logic of price and the familiar and well understood even if not perfectly realistic classical market concept. As a phenomenon it raises questions leading to the FME investigations that follow.

Since market mythology deals much with "optimum," "social maximum" and the like, it has been suitable to include some part of an essay, making the last chapter, which had been contributed to a symposium dealing with such terms. Out of respect for the flood of writings and applications I have added a note[9] on the – now not always known or remembered – beginnings of "data envelope analysis" and production efficiency measurement where I had part, as author of the frontier and stochastic-frontier production functions.

Different parts of the book have passages in common. This happens because they were prepared originally for different occasions without a view of their coming together in a volume. Such repetitions, which could now have been eliminated, are sometimes retained in order to preserve original character, or the effect of a combination.

8 Though Susan Senior assures me IPE is well established as "International Political Economy" this is an indispensable local use.
9 Note 4: Historical note on "Data Envelope Analysis" : frontier and stochastic-frontier production functions.

Acknowledgements

I have to acknowledge with thanks my debt to Jim Alvey, of Macquarie University, NSW, for many discussions and drawing my attention to the article of J. M. Keynes of 1933 important for the last part of the book, "On Trade, and Self-sufficiency".

I am also indebted to Ginette Benoit of the Canadian Institute for Research on Regional Development, Moncton NB, for her much appreciated editing of an earlier version prepared for the 1991 Symposium on "Equity and Efficiency in Economic Development" in honour of Benjamin Higgins.

The "Market & Myth" part which here comes before that part in fact happened afterwards, when I was recently at Bilkent University, Ankara. There I have been indebted to Nedim Alemdar, and to Tuvana Demirden and Ivan Pastine, for frequent discussions besides some reading and commentary – and to Ali Doğramacı and Sübidey Togan for the accident of my being at Bilkent.

I acknowledge with pleasure my similar indebtedness to Mario Bunge, of McGill University, Montreal, for many related discussions going over many years, and now also to Luigi Luini and Susan Senior in Siena. I am compelled to mention Kumaraswamy Velupillai and Steven Lukes since with them my favourite composition "Market & Myth" got some distinct approval.

Finally, I thank Robert Langham and Terry Clague of Routledge very much for their collaboration that has made a most welcome conclusion for the project.

Part I
The market phenomenon

The market is a distinct phenomenon present in all kinds of circumstances. To understand it as such, and as being unconditioned by very special circumstances, it should in some way be cut off for a separate treatment. Though one may then be in an imaginary world, demonstrating the market phenomenon in a well-defined, abstract world – one we know well because we invented it – should go some way towards providing an explanation of the phenomenon.

The occurrence of markets is commonplace, it is outstanding, no planning committee or other agency is required to take part, they just happen, almost anywhere. The conditions to be considered therefore should be quite primitive, and for developing a theory some such conditions have to be explored.

The possibility of a market cannot be isolated from the process of original realization. An existing possible arrangement is tantalizing in the absence of a way of getting to it, from some, and perhaps any position. The *tâtonnement* or tentative groping process of Walras, or something like it, is therefore an essential part of the matter. The pure existence possibility has to be joined with some operational finding process. That requires a kind of roughness, overriding disturbances, so as to embody the stability of the self-regulated system without which it could not, in practice, exist.

The considerations are necessarily abstract, intended only to reflect something of the *form* of common experience. A simplest representation therefore could be of adequate value. This is not micro-economic theory that pretends to offer a picture of the system built from ultimate parts, but more on the surface.

That a good has a price P is demonstrated when a transaction takes place, in which it has that price. There is no real alternative sense in which a good can have a price. It means nothing that cabbages are $1 per pound if no one, or rather no two, are buying and selling at that price. Goods left on the shelf with a price tag on them, like many a house for sale, do not have a price until they are sold. Those tags are at most offers, or just factors in the *tâtonnement*. There are countless other goods on the shelf, some of them not yet invented.

In the transaction there is a buyer and a seller, and, even though two are present, *what is bought and what is sold are the same thing*. There seems to be no escape from that. In other words, *supply S equals demand D*: $S = D$. This is *not an equation with content*. It just connects two names that have been given to the same thing. But why give the same object two different names? It would be more logical to give it one, say the *transaction quantity Q*.

We have a transaction price P and quantity Q for a good. Both are observable, and they are observed together. But it is very popular to give Q two different names, S and D, and then talk about S and D separately as if they were distinct entities, which could, moreover, exist apart. There is a puzzle here, or some confusion – possibly on the part of this writer.

It could be wondered (from limitless curiosity) why any price should be just P and not higher or lower. Since the market is central to economics, it is in some way understandable that there should be an attempt to give an explanation of price, even a complete one. But what kind of explanation can there be? To explain a change in a price is a more modest endeavour than explaining a price. The same is true with regard to the neck of the giraffe, the elongation is well understood in terms of evolutionary mechanisms (despite some debate about that) but no biologist attempts a complete explanation of the giraffe. Economists, of the fundamentalist kind, have greater courage. They offer an explanation of price, of all prices; or, rather, a form for an explanation has been proposed (perhaps more than one). But carrying out a realization of the form is a further matter having much less attention. One may ask what content there could be just in the proposal about form, and whether there is anything in it that can be known to be true or false, or neither.

A main doctrine about a price in settled times was that it should be settled. A price was part of the order of things like fowls of the air and beasts of the field; there was such a thing as a proper chicken and it had a proper price. The price could be known and counted on; it could enter into plans for a dinner or the allocation of a budget. This is a rational position, and practical, but it is not one that can always be enjoyed, because unsettled times produce changes also in prices. The interest then is still practical; not why prices should all be absolutely what they are, but how they might change. This is as with the giraffe. There can still be the question of why there should be any offer to explain all prices, and even whether there really is an explanation.

It has been said "Teach a parrot to say "Supply and Demand" and there you have an economist" (Stephen Leacock, *Literary Lapses*). Whether or not this statement deserves approval it suggests a pleonasm, since we decided that, to the extent of anything visible, supply and demand are the same thing. They are not equal, but are indistinguishable. That is a matter of inescapable logic, since what means buying something to a buyer means selling something to a seller, and *these two things happen to be identical*. All the same, though the two things are one, it is outstanding that the same cannot be said of the buyer and the seller. These are two separate individuals. In fact, since the transaction is voluntary on both sides, it seems something of a coincidence that they got together. For theory, here is not just the chance but the matter to be explained.

This apparent chance has an extension to the aggregate, where it looks as if an unlikely coincidence must occur in order to have a price at all, because those willing to buy must be exactly matched by those willing to sell. It seems implausible that everyday economic life, where the price phenomenon is a commonplace, should be based on such a precarious balance. Theory should deal with the possibility of the fine arrangement; and, since feasibility is of incomplete interest without an idea of how it is realized, it should deal also with the process for arriving at it. Just now, however, the concern is with elements rather than aggregates.

The encounter between buyer and seller might in reality have some significant effect on each. If this is of a special and individual kind it must be ignored, and for purposes of theory we should deal with simple automata. A simplicity in the encounter is assured if the only recognizable interface between buyer and seller is the price. For a start, it is supposed that the buyer and the seller in their separateness each have a definite potentiality for their part in the transaction which takes place, already existing and then realized from the encounter. A shape for such assumptions is provided by the following:

i   Anyone willing to buy a unit of a good at some price would be willing to buy it also at any lower price.
ii Anyone willing to sell a unit of a good at some price would be willing to sell it also at any higher price.

These are norms consistent with price being an incentive to sell and a disincentive to buy, and not necessarily absolute laws. We know from Veblen about ostentatious expenditure, and ostentatious charity or any other dispositions that might be imagined could be an addition to that. The situation is not different from Newton's when he made uniform motion a norm; so non-uniform motion causes attention to forces, if any can be found, and here ostentation is to Veblen something like what gravitation was to Newton. These assumptions express *free disposal*: the buyer who pays less is free to dispose of the difference leaving a situation which is the same and therefore as acceptable as when more had been paid, and similarly on the side of a seller.

If P_b is the upper limit to prices at which the buyer would be willing to buy a unit and P_s is the lower limit at which the seller would sell, then simultaneous willingness on both sides requires

$$P_s < P < P_d.$$

Hence

$$P_s < P_d,$$

for simultaneous consent to a transaction quantity at some price P, which then can be anywhere between P_s and P_d. Otherwise, at least one refuses and there is no transaction.

When successive further units are brought in we get declining and rising step functions, and if the units are small and numerous these become general monotonic curves, the supply and demand curves for buyer and seller. This line can be taken further by bringing in notions about a market and these individuals being in one.

Important data of the sensible world of economics concern form, not hard to get but evident from experience. No measurements are needed to know it, or read it. Also, things on paper are a part of economics because they affect behaviour and events; they are a real part of the real world. There is a voluminous recording and manipulation of data, but nothing of what in the main passes for economic theory really depends on it; in part of its nature it is near to ritual, in some form indispensable to social decision making as from time immemorial. The empiricism of natural scientists is different from so-called 'empirical work' in economics.

These possible views are entertained in connection with price theory based on supply and demand, in order to evaluate rather than object to it. The theory relies on ideas of the kind already described that have obvious reference to experience and we know what they mean. But there is a transition at some point, and there can be questions about the result. For instance, if the final theory were true there would be no way of knowing it, and so there can be question about the sense of offering it as true, or even as possibly true. As for its being false, in particular economies we know that it is, at least to some extent, because for instance prices are subject to various regulations. Also, time is a complication that makes the theory even more difficult to interpret. Nonetheless, and perhaps rightly so, the theory of prices and their equilibrium (in an unknown and unknowable framework) is given an important place in economic theory. Whether or not there should be a complaint exactly here, there can be one of another order about the 'welfare' appendages to this theory.

The matters up to now have a local and individual reference, but dealing with an economy signifies a global framework of information and competition. Stephen Leacock brings that out in 'Boarding House Geometry', another of his *Literary Lapses*. He sets out the argument in the manner of Euclid, a few Postulates and then Propositions. The former go something like this:

Postulates

A landlady is an angular figure equal to anything.

Boarding house sheets produced however far each way will not meet.

A pie is produced any number of times

. . .

and so forth. Then comes the first Proposition, and its Proof:

Proposition   All boarding house rents are equal.

Proof is by the method of *reduction ad absurdum* by which an hypothesis is impossible if it has impossible consequences:

Proof   Suppose, if possible, that the rents are not equal. Then one is greater than the other. Then the other is less than it might have been, which is absurd, &c.   □

The absurdity is from the landlady's side and it could have gone just as well from the tenant's side – that is, the other is greater than it might have been . . . Leacock takes for granted our stated assumptions about buyers and sellers. While there are transactions in a good at price P no seller will sell at a lower price and no buyer will buy at a higher one. Since joint consent is needed, there will be no transactions at a price above or below P, and the good has a single price P. There is a global equalization, a global information situation having been presupposed.

Should buyers willing to buy at the price be exhausted before sellers willing to sell, then if further transactions take place they will be at a price that brings in more buyers and thereby a lower price, though not one so low as to cut out all sellers. Those sellers who are within their threshold and prepared to sell at a lower price will take part, and those others who were at or beyond it will not. In going to a lower price demand rises and supply falls; similarly with the reverse situation, in which further transactions would take place, if at all, at a higher price. At any point the price is what it is because all who would be buyers at that price find sellers and all sellers, buyers. There might be none of either. But it makes no sense to say cabbages are £1 per kilo if there is a would-be buyer at the price who cannot find a seller, or a seller who cannot find a buyer. The price being P depends on the balance $S = D$. If both sides of this equation are zero, as when buyers and sellers are far apart and there are none for a range of prices, it would not be precarious; otherwise it is, and there are movements. This is a dynamic picture giving sense to movements. It does not depend on a knowledge of the total numbers that would buy or sell at whatever price; whatever these might be, should it make sense even to refer to them, they can be recognized to be continually changing. At any moment one can in principle know the prevailing price P and the transaction quantity Q which is simultaneously both supply and demand, and that is all.

The theory of price as determined by the equality of supply and demand postulates that supply and demand are functions

$$S = S(P), \qquad D = D(P)$$

of the possible price P, and the prevailing price P is determined by the condition $S(P) = D(P)$. If this theory is offered as having an empirical basis, there is a problem about knowledge of these functions, since only one point is observable on each, the point (P, Q). If the price P ever changes, it must be because the functions have changed and so are no longer observable; instead, a new single point can be observed on the new 'functions'. *If the functions do not change they cannot be observed and if they do change they cannot be observed either.*

The market in which goods have a price at which they are bought and sold is a commonplace phenomenon. With it there can be the idea, even if not the exact experience, of a settled market where, day after day, the prices and transaction quantities are the same. If we can think of a market as we do because of experience, we can also think of a settled market. It is a logical possibility arising from the terms of description of markets, and it makes an ideal reference.

With a settled market, the possibility can be entertained of its being made up of settled individuals with fixed supply and demand functions. That is an imaginable possibility, in fact, one that is already imagined in price theory. A market of some sort is known to be a real possibility in some real circumstances. Now it can be asked if a market is a possibility in some ideally possible circumstances with fair provisos that do not ask anything positively wrong from experience. This is an important first question for a theoretical understanding of the market system. A negative answer would be a great surprise and would make the market phenomenon thoroughly mysterious. Markets are found everywhere, in principle self created and self governed without any centralized intervention; and one would have to wonder what it is in the real world and not in the imagined world that makes them possible. With a positive answer there is, in addition to peace of mind, a central finding about the nature of markets, showing the known real possibility matched by an intrinsic theoretical possibility.

To develop the question, consider functions which give the vector S of differences between aggregate supply and aggregate demand for all goods as determined by the vector p of all the prices. These are *market functions*, given in the form of *excess supply functions*, so

$$D(p) = -S(p)$$

would be *excess demand functions*.

In principle, the economy is composed of individuals each with such a function $s(p)$, and the market function S is a sum of all the individual functions s. At any prices, each individual buys some goods and sells others, paying for purchases with receipts from sales, so that demands match supplies in exchange value and there is the individual *budget constraint* $ps(p) = 0$. Then for their sum $S = \sum s$, we have $pS(p) = 0$ which is called *Walras' Law*.

The prices $p > 0$ are significant only as determining exchange rates between goods from their ratios. Since the functions s depend only on the ratios, we have $s(tp) = s(p)$ for all $t > 0$. Summing, the function $S(p)$ is defined for all $p > 0$ and such that

$$pS(p) = 0, \qquad S(tp) = S(p) \quad (t > 0).$$

The market feasibility question, or the existence of some feasible prices, is now the question of whether or not there exist some prices $p > 0$ for which aggregate supply equals aggregate demand for every good, or the excess supplies are simultaneously all zero, that is,

$$S(p) = 0.$$

It is not enough to know that such prices should exist; a further issue is how they would be found. After all, no one is doing the computing but the economy itself. The *Law of Supply and Demand*, that the price of a good falls if it is in excess supply and rises if it is in excess demand, is an available principle which, put in a suitable form, should amount to a computational algorithm.

Excess supply or demand is known not by a fixed identifiable individual or agency, but in a scattered decentralized way, as soon as a buyer of a good cannot find a seller, or a seller a buyer at the price of the last transaction. That price then is no longer the price. The possible price rises or falls, in the minds and readiness of unfulfilled buyers or sellers in the one case or the other, until a transaction takes place, when it becomes the actual price; and so forth. A consistency with this picture is required; it is not exactly the *tâtonnement* of Walras, but more or less the same – and there is no need for the usual auctioneer.

Part II

Market equilibrium and stability

1 INTRODUCTION

This treatment of general equilibrium maintains the view (in complete agreement with Schumpeter) that the topic has most essentially to do with aggregates, and any modelling of underlying elements, in particular anything to do with utility, is secondary if not spurious.

The approach proceeds from the usual basic model where

a1   excess supply depends on prices to the extent of their ratios, which determine exchange rates,

which is joined with

a2   continuity,

and

a3   Walras' Law, which expresses the aggregate budget constraint, by which what is bought in any transaction is paid for out of what is sold.

In other words, we have an exchange economy, where prices are significant to the extent of their ratios, which specify exchange rates between goods.

An additional assumption, belonging to the approach to be made, is

b1   *Finite Supply Capacity*, that the excess supply for any good is bounded from above.

This could come from physical limitation of production possibilities.

There is also

b2   the *Intercept Condition*, that demand for a good must exceed supply if the price is small, or that demand overtakes supply of a good as its price falls, to make excess supply negative.

This is consistent with the principle that the price of a good is an incentive to sell and a disincentive to buy, so that as it falls supply decreases and demand increases so as eventually to overtake supply.

Assumptions a1, a2, a3 *with* b1, b2 *are enough to assure the existence of equilibrium prices.* The proof uses the KKM Lemma, dealt with in Appendix II.

One further assumption provides for global stability under a differential price adjustment process, and hence uniqueness of the equilibrium. This is

b3   the *Slope Condition*, which requires excess supply of a good to be decreasing as a function of the other prices.

It will be seen that *the Slope Condition*, which assures the global stability of an equilibrium, *implies the Intercept Condition*, which already serves for the existence of an equilibrium.

The sense of the Slope Condition is that there is incentive to buy more and sell less of a good if the price of another good increases. Behind this is the idea that the less bought of the other good, as by the already mentioned incentive principle, is offset by more bought of the first; and similarly with the supply side.

The method for the stability proof involves algebra of distribution matrices given in Appendix III. These matrices occur as transition matrices in Markov process theory where stability depends on convergence of infinite powers, whereas here the convergence is for infinite products.

2   DESCRIPTIVE FUNCTIONS

Market excess supply functions $S(p) \in \mathbf{R}^n$ are defined for all $p > 0$, $p \in \mathbf{R}_n$. The market as a sum of independent individuals requires the function S for the market to be a sum of functions s for the individuals,

$$S(p) = \sum s(p),$$

where, since prices are significant to the extent of determining exchange rates,

$$s(tp) = s(p) \quad (t > 0), \tag{i}$$

and since $s(p)$ represents an exchange of goods at these rates,

$$ps(p) = 0. \tag{ii}$$

Hence, by summation,

$$S(tp) = S(p) \quad (t > 0) \tag{i'}$$
$$pS(p) = 0 \qquad \text{(Walras' Law)} \tag{ii'}$$

For the vector $e = e(p)$ of *market value functions*

$$e_j = p_j S_j(p),$$

which give excess supplies in money or exchange value terms, it follows that

$$e(tp) = te(p) \quad (t > 0), \qquad\qquad\qquad\qquad\qquad\qquad (i)''$$

$$\sum_j e_j(p) = 0. \qquad\qquad\qquad\qquad\qquad\qquad\qquad (ii)''$$

From (i) the market functions, defined for $p > 0$, are completely specified from their values in the interior of the *normalized price simplex*:

$$\Delta = \left\{ p : p > 0, \sum p_i = 1 \right\},$$

where prices sum to 1. The *supply capacity limits are*

$$u_j = \sup S_j(p),$$

and the *Finite Supply Capacity Condition* requires

$$u_j < \infty.$$

Joining (i) and (ii) with this assumption, together with continuity of the S_j, *the value functions e are continuous and bounded above in* Δ. But from (ii)'',

$$e_j = -\sum_{i \neq j} e_i,$$

so *also they are bounded below*; this still allows the S_j to be unbounded below, from demand being insatiable. Hence, being bounded and continuous, *the functions e have unique continuous extensions to the closure of* Δ.

The *Intercept Condition* requires that, for any p_i ($i \neq j$),

$$S_j < 0 \quad \text{for small } p_i,$$

equivalently, on Δ,

$$p_j = 0 \Rightarrow e_j < 0.$$

The sense of this condition is that demand overtakes supply of a good as its price goes to zero. Then from (ii)'',

$$p_j = 1 \Rightarrow p_i = 0 \quad (i \neq j)$$

$$\Rightarrow e_j = -\sum_{i \neq j} e_i > 0,$$

so we also have

$$p_j = 1 \Rightarrow e_j > 0.$$

With the continuity, it follows from Bolzano's Theorem[1] that

$$e_j = 0, \quad \text{for some } p_j, \quad 0 < p_j < 1,$$

in which case also

$$S_j = 0, \quad \text{for some } p_j, \quad 0 < p_j < 1.$$

Thus, other prices being fixed, any one market for a good can be cleared by setting its price.[2]

3   EXISTENCE THEOREM

For general equilibrium, all markets have to be cleared simultaneously, that is,

$$S = 0, \quad \text{for some } p > 0.$$

As to be seen, the available assumptions already imply this is possible.
   Consider continuous excess supply value functions

$$e_j = p_j S_j(p),$$

defined on the normalized prices simplex Δ such that

$$\sum_j e_j = 0,$$

and

$$p_j = 0 \Rightarrow e_j < 0,$$

that is, satisfying Walras' Law and the Intercept Condition. We will show that $S_j(p) = 0$ for all j, for some $p > 0$.

---

1 A continuous function defined on a interval takes every value between any two of its values. Hence if it is positive and negative it must also be zero at some point.
2 Prices being significant to the extent of their ratios, one price varying while others remain fixed can mean that, as the one varies in the interval [0, 1], the others vary to preserve normalization while their ratios remain fixed. In other words, there is movement on a line connecting a vertex of the normalized price simplex Δ to a point in the opposite face.

Let

$$C_j = \{p: e_j \geq 0\},$$

so these are closed sets since the functions e_j are continuous, and for any subset V of the goods, or of vertices of the simplex, let

$$C_V = \bigcup_{j \in V} C_j.$$

The face of the simplex on the vertices V is

$$\Delta_V = \{p: j \in \overline{V} \Rightarrow p_j = 0\}.$$

It will be shown that

$$\Delta_V \subset C_V \quad \text{for all } V,$$

and hence, by the KKM Lemma of Appendix II,

$$\bigcap_j C_j \neq O.$$

But any

$$p \in \bigcap_j C_j$$

is by definition such that

$$e_j(p) \geq 0 \quad \text{for all } j.$$

But since

$$\sum_j e_j = 0,$$

this is equivalent to

$$e_j(p) = 0 \quad \text{for all } j.$$

By the Intercept Condition this implies $p > 0$ and so is equivalent to

$$S_j(p) = 0 \quad \text{for all } j,$$

as required.

Thus, for any $p \in \Delta$,

$$p \in \Delta_V \Leftrightarrow j \in \overline{V} \Rightarrow p_j = 0 \qquad \because \text{ definition of the left}$$
$$\Rightarrow j \in \overline{V} \Rightarrow e_j \leq 0 \qquad \because \text{ Intercept Condition}$$
$$\Rightarrow \sum_{j \in \overline{V}} e_j \leq 0 \qquad \because \text{ inequality sum}$$
$$\Leftrightarrow \sum_{j \in V} e_j \geq 0 \qquad \because \text{ Walras' Law}$$
$$\Rightarrow e_j \geq 0 \quad \text{for some } j \in V \quad \because \text{ inequality sum}$$
$$\Leftrightarrow p \in C_j \quad \text{for some } j \in V \quad \because \text{ definition of } C_j$$
$$\Leftrightarrow p \in C_V \qquad \because \text{ definition of } C_V$$

$$\therefore \Delta_V \subset C_V. \qquad \square$$

4   STABILITY THEOREM

There is also the question of how the prices may be found, by a process that takes place within the economy arising from reactions to the shortages and surpluses that occur. The imbalances between buyers and sellers produce *market forces* which adjust prices upwards and downwards according to the *Law of Supply and Demand*, and should lead towards proper market prices, these making an *equilibrium* for the adjustment process. Hence there is the question of the stability of the system, in regard to a model for such forces.

Such a model is provided by the differential adjustment process

$$\dot{p} = f(p)$$

where

$$f_j(p) = -v_j e_j(p) \quad (v_j > 0).$$

One further assumption provides for global stability under such an adjustment process, and uniqueness of equilibrium. This is the *Slope Condition*, which requires $S_j(p)$, and equivalently e_j, to be decreasing in $p_i (i \neq j)$. From (ii), with this condition, e is increasing in p_j.

Suppose market functions e_j are continuously differentiable and such that

$$e_{ij} = \frac{\partial e_i}{\partial p_j} < 0 \quad (j \neq i).$$

This is a consequence of the Slope Condition which, though different, is similar to the already familiar gross-substitutes condition on excess demand.

Now from Walras' Law

$$\sum_j e_j = 0,$$

we have

$$\sum_i e_{ij} = 0,$$

and so also $e_{ii} \geq 0$. Because the e_i are homogeneous of degree 1 they satisfy Euler's identity

$$\sum_j e_{ij} p_j = e_i,$$

with the consequence that $e_i < 0$ if $p_i = 0$. Thus, *the Slope Condition implies the Intercept Condition*, and so, by the theorem of the last section, we have the existence of $\bar{p} > 0$ for which

$$e_i(\bar{p}) = 0 \quad \text{for all } i.$$

We will also be able to deduce the uniqueness of such $\bar{p}$ from the following stability considerations.

Consider now the differential price adjustment system

$$\dot{p}_i = -v_i e_i(p),$$

where the *reaction coefficients*, or velocities, are any constants $v_i > 0$. Since replacing p_i by p_i / v_i corresponds to a change of the arbitrary physical units, we can suppose the change already made, so in effect the coefficients v_i all become equal to 1 and the system becomes simply

$$\dot{p} = -e(p).$$

Given any initial $p(0)$ in the interior of Δ, this has a unique solution $p(t)$ ($t \geq 0$), and the Intercept Condition assures us that this remains in the interior of Δ. We want to show that

$$p(t) \to \bar{p}(t \to \infty).$$

In other words, $\bar{p}$ is a globally stable equilibrium, in the differential adjustment process, and hence also the unique equilibrium.

For a small time interval τ the adjustment process is approximated by the finite difference system

$$p' - p = -\tau e(p),$$

where p becomes p' after time τ. Thus we have $p' = f(p)$ where

$$f(p) = p - \tau e(p),$$

so $e(\bar{p}) = 0$ is equivalent to $f(\bar{p}) = \bar{p}$.

For the derivatives of f_i we have

$$f_{ii} = 1 - \tau e_{ii}, \qquad f_{ij} = -\tau e_{ij} > 0 \quad (j \neq i),$$

and

$$\sum_i f_{ij} = 1 - \tau \sum_i e_{ij} = 1.$$

Thus the derivative matrix g of f is a positive row distribution matrix provided

$$\tau < 1/e_{ii}.$$

From continuity of the derivatives and compactness of Δ, τ can be made small enough to make this so for all p. Then with g positive and continuous, and Δ compact, the elements of g have a lower bound $\mu > 0$.

Now consider the r-fold iterated image

$$f^{(r)}(p) = f(f(\dots f(p)\dots)),$$

that is,

$$f^{(0)}(p) = p, \qquad f^{(r)}(p) = f\left(f^{(r-1)}(p)\right) \quad (r = 1, 2, \dots).$$

The derivative matrix, by the chain rule, is

$$g^{(r)} = g^1 \dots g^r,$$

where g^s is g evaluated at $f^{(s-1)}(p)$. Then, by the theorem of Appendix III, Corollary, for all $p, q \in \Delta$,

$$\left|(q - p)g^{(r)}\right| < |q - p|(1 - \mu)^r.$$

But by the theorem of the Mean,

$$f^{(r)}(q) - f^{(r)}(p) = (q - p)g^{(r)}(z),$$

where $z \in \langle p, q \rangle$. We can now conclude that, for any $\varepsilon > 0$, there exists s such that, for all $p, q \in \Delta$,

$$\left|f^{(r)}(q) - f^{(r)}(p)\right| < \varepsilon$$

for all $r > s$, and hence that $f^{(r)}(p)(r \to \infty)$ converges to a constant function with the single value $\bar{p}$, since in any case this must be one of its values. In other words, $\bar{p}$ is a stable equilibrium in the finite adjustment system $p' = f(p)$.

The differential system and the finite difference systems have the same equilibria. The finite difference systems are stable and approximate the differential system for small τ. It follows that the differential system is also stable.

Appendices

I SPERNER'S LEMMA

Let S be a simplex and V the set of its vertices, these being $n + 1$ in number if S has dimension n, making it an n-simplex. Taking barycentric coordinates with S as simplex of reference, any point $x \in S$ has coordinates x_i $(i = 1, \ldots, n)$ where

$$x_i \geq 0, \quad \sum_i x_i = 1.$$

Thus vertex j of S has coordinates

$$x_i = 0 \quad (i \neq j), \qquad x_j = 1.$$

A *face* of S is a simplex whose vertices are a subset of the vertices of S. The vertices of S are the faces of dimension 0, and S itself is the only face of dimension n. The 1-faces or *edges* are the line segments joining pairs of vertices.

A *simplicial dissection* of S is a collection T of simplices covering S any pair of which are either disjoint or have a common face for their intersection. The vertices of T include all the vertices of its simplices, and so also all the vertices of S. A dissection T of S provides a dissection also of the faces of S, whose simplices are faces of the simplices of T. By dissecting the simplices of a dissection T of S we have a further dissection of S, whose vertices contain the vertices of T as a subset.

The *barycentric subdivision* of a simplex S is the particular simplicial dissection $B(S)$ whose vertices are the vertices of S together with the bisectors of the edges. Barycentric subdivision can also apply to any dissection. By n-times repeated subdivision, we have the nth barycentric subdivision $B(\ldots B(S) \ldots)$ of S, whose simplices have edges which are $1/2^n$ of the edges of S.

The *carrier face* of any point of S is the face of lowest dimension which contains it. Thus, $V_x = \{i : x_i > 0\}$ is the set of vertices of the carrier face S_x of x. The vertices of S are their own carrier faces. Also, any face of a simplex of a dissection has a carrier face, which is the face of lowest dimension of the base simplex which carries all its vertices.

A *Sperner label* for a point of S can be any vertex of its carrier face. Thus, L is a Sperner label for x if $L \in V_x$, that is, if $x_L > 0$. In particular, the only possible Sperner label for a vertex of S is the vertex itself. A *Sperner labelling* for a simplicial dissection T of S is a function L which assigns a Sperner label $L(x)$ to every vertex x of T. Then a *Sperner simplex* is a simplex of T whose vertex labels describe all the vertices of S.

Theorem (Sperner)   For any simplex S and any simplicial dissection T of S, and any Sperner labelling of the vertices of T, the number of Sperner simplices is odd, and consequently there exists at least one.

First we will see what it means for a 1-simplex S, with vertices 0, 1. This is a line segment with 0, 1 as endpoints, say on the left and right.

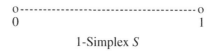

1-Simplex S

For a simplicial dissection T of S the vertices are a set of points of S including 0 and 1. Neighbouring ones join in segments, which are the simplices of the dissection T. These cover S, and any pair either are disjoint or have a face, in this case an endpoint, in common.

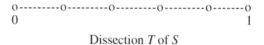

Dissection T of S

S itself is the carrier face of every vertex of T except its own vertices, which carry themselves. Therefore, with a Sperner labelling they carry either 0 or 1 as labels, while the vertices of S label themselves.

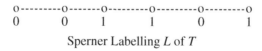

Sperner Labelling L of T

A Sperner simplex is a segment whose vertex labels include both 0 and 1. It is clear that one must exist in this special case. Scanning the vertices of T from the left, we start with a 0. Succeeding ones carry labels 0 or 1, but the last has the label 1. The first 1 that occurs produces the first Sperner simplex. Since there is a vertex which carries the label 1, the last being a case, so that a 1 must be encountered sooner or later, at least one Sperner simplex exists. The argument of the theorem is that the number of Sperner simplices is odd, so there must be at least one. We can see that in this case. In scanning the vertices from the left, every alternation of labels produces a Sperner simplex. Starting from label 0, any number of alternations that ends with a 1 must be odd, and we do end with a 1 on the right. Therefore, the number of Sperner simplices is odd.

For the general proof of the theorem, the method is by induction on the simplex dimension n. The case $n = 0$ is true, vacuously. We have, moreover, just given an independent proof for $n = 1$. Suppose now that the theorem is true for dimension

$n - 1$, and consider a simplex S of dimension n. Let T be a simplicial dissection of S, and let L be a Sperner labelling of T. These induce the same on every face of S, to which the inductive hypothesis applies. Therefore, every face of S contains a simplex, a face of some simplex of T, whose vertex labels exactly describe its vertices; moreover, there is an odd number of such simplices in any face. The proof of the theorem has two parts and we use this consequence of the inductive hypothesis in the second.

Consider the class C of faces of T with vertex labels $1, \ldots, n$. Any one is a face of a simplex of T whose remaining vertex label is either 0 or different from 0 and so among $1, \ldots, n$. Let N be the number of simplices of T with labels $0, 1, \ldots, n$. These are the Sperner simplices. Also let N' be the number of simplices of T with labels $1, \ldots, n$ and another repeating one of these. Each of the N has one face of class C and each of the N' has two. Thus the number of occurrences of a simplex of class C as a face of some simplex of T is $N + 2N'$.

Now, further, each C-simplex is counted once if it is in a face of S, since then it is a face of just one simplex of T, and otherwise twice, since then it is a face of two simplices of T. But a C-simplex in the face $1, \ldots, n$ of S is a Sperner simplex for that face, and by the inductive hypothesis the number of these is odd. Also, a C-simplex cannot lie in any other face, by the Sperner labelling rule. Thus an odd number M of faces of T have been counted once in the total $N + 2N'$ and the remaining ones, say M', have been counted twice. Thus, we have

$$N + 2N' = M + 2M',$$

where M is odd. It follows that N is odd. $\qquad\square$

II THE KKM LEMMA

Lemma If U is compact and closed subsets $F_i \subset U$ are such that

$$\bigcap_i F_i = O,$$

then, there exists $\varepsilon > 0$ such that, for any X, if

$$X \cap F_i \neq O,$$

for all i, then X has diameter at least ε.

The set $\otimes_i F_i$ is compact, and the function

$$f(x) = \min_{ij} |x_i - x_j| \quad (x_i \in F_i)$$

defined on it is continuous and so attains a minimum ε, where $\varepsilon > 0$ since $\bigcap_i F_i = O$. Hence for any $a, a \in X \cap F_i$, for all i implies that the diameter of X is

$$\sup \{|x - y| : x, y \in X\} \geq f(a) \geq \varepsilon,$$

so it is at least ε. $\qquad\square$

Theorem (Knaster–Kuratowski–Mazurkiewicz)   If S is a simplex, S_v the face on any subset v of vertices, F_i a closed subset associated with any vertex i, and

$$F_v = \bigcup_{i \in v} F_i$$

and if $S_v \subset F_v$ for all v, then

$$\bigcap_i F_i \neq O.$$

Suppose if possible that $\bigcap_i F_i = O$ and let $\varepsilon > 0$ be as in the Lemma. Consider a simplicial subdivision T of S where the simplices have diameter $< \varepsilon$. For any vertex t of T let v be the set of vertices of the carrier face of S, so that $t \in S_v \subset F_v$ and hence $t \in F_i$ for some i. Let $L(t) = i$. Then L is a Sperner labelling of the vertices of T. Hence by Sperner's Lemma there exists a simplex X of T such that, for all i, $L(t) = i$ for some vertex t of X, so $X \cap F_i \neq O$ for all i. But by the Lemma this is impossible since X has diameter less than ε. Hence the hypothesis is impossible. $\qquad\qquad\square$

III   DISTRIBUTION MATRICES

A *distribution* on n objects is a set of n numbers which are non-negative and sum to 1. A *distribution vector* is any vector whose elements form a distribution. Introducing I to denote a column vector of any order with elements all 1, the condition for a row vector p to be a distribution vector can be stated as

$$p \geq 0, \quad \text{as } pI = 1.$$

Then

$$\Delta = \{p \colon p \geq 0, \, pI = 1\}$$

is the $(n - 1)$-simplex of distribution vectors of order n.

A row (or column) *distribution matrix* is any matrix whose rows (or columns) are each given by a distribution vector. Any product ab of distribution matrices a, b is again a distribution matrix. The condition for a matrix a to be a distribution matrix can be stated as

$$a \geq 0, \quad aI = I,$$

the orders of the Is here being different, unless a is square, in which case a can be regarded as a mapping

$$a : \Delta \to \Delta$$

of the simplex Δ into itself where any point $p \in \Delta$ has image $pa \in \Delta$. For if $q = pa$ then we have $q \geq 0$ because $p \geq 0$, $a \geq 0$. Also, because $pI = 1$, $aI = I$, we have

$$qI = (pa)I = p(aI) = pI = 1,$$

so $qI = 1$. Hence also $q \in \Delta$.

  Let Λ be the set of displacements in Δ, so

$$\Lambda = \{q - p: p, q \in \Delta\},$$

and

$$v \in L \Leftrightarrow vI = 0.$$

For any $v \in \Lambda$ let

$$|v| = \sum_i |v_i|,$$

so

$$|v| \geq 0, \qquad |v| = 0 \Leftrightarrow v = 0.$$

If a is a distribution matrix, and $v \in \Lambda$, then also $va \in \Lambda$. From $aI = I$ we have

$$(va)I = v(aI) = vI.$$

So from $vI = 0$, also $(va)I = 0$, and so we can consider also $|va|$.

Theorem   If a is a distribution matrix and a_k is the smallest element in column k, and if v is any vector for which $vI = 0$, then

$$|va| \leq |v|(1 - a_k).$$

 It can be taken that

  i $\sum_i v_i a_{ik} \geq 0$

since otherwise v can be replaced by $-v$. Now we have

  ii $a \geq 0$

  iii $aI = I$ and definitions of $|v|$ and a_k

  iv $vI = 0$

so that

$$|va| = \sum_{j \neq k} \left| \sum_i v_i a_{ik} \right| + \sum_i v_i a_{ik} \qquad \because \text{(i)}$$

$$\leq \sum_{j \neq k} \sum_i |v_i| a_{ij} + \sum_i v_i a_{ik} \qquad \because \text{(ii)}$$

$$= \sum_j \sum_i |v_i| a_{ij} - \sum_i (|v_i| - v_i) a_{ik}$$

$$\leq |v| - \sum_i (|v_i| - v_i) a_k \qquad \because \text{(iii)}$$

$$= |v|(1 - a_k) \qquad \because \text{(iv)}$$

$$\therefore \quad |va| \leq |v|(1 - a_k) \qquad \qquad \square$$

Corollary If also $g^1, \ldots, g^r$ are distribution matrices and μ is a lower bound for their elements, then

$$|vg^1 \ldots g^r| \leq |v|(1 - \mu)^r.$$

Bibliography

Afriat, S. N. (1987). *Logic of Choice and Economic Theory*. Oxford: Clarendon Press.

Allingham, Michael (1972). Tatonnement stability: an econometric approach. *Econometrica* 40, 27–41.

—— (1973). Equilibrium and Disequilibrium. Cambridge, Mass.: Ballinger.

—— (1974). Equilibrium and stability. *Econometrica* 42, 705–16. Reprinted in Blaug and Hoover (Eds) *Critical Ideas in Economics*. E. Elgar, 1999.

—— (1975). *General Equilibrium*. London: Macmillan.

—— (1989). *Theory of Markets*. London: Macmillan.

Arrow, Kenneth J. and G. Debreu (1954). Existence of equilibrium for a competitive economy. *Econometrica* 22, 265–90.

—— and F. H. Hahn (1971). *General Competitive Analysis*. San Francisco: Holden-Day.

Debreu, G. (1959). *Theory of Value: An Axiomatic Analysis of Economic Equilibrium*. Cowles Foundation Monograph no. 17. New York: John Wiley.

Knaster, B., K. Kuratowski and S. Mazurkiewiez (1931). Ein Beweis des Fixpunktsatzes für n-dimensionale Simplexe. *Fundamenta Mathematica* 14, 132–7.

McKenzie, Lionel W. (1954). On equilibrium in Graham's model of world trade and other competitive systems. *Econometrica* 22, 147–61.

—— (1959). On the existence of general equilibrium for a competitive market. *Econometrica* 27, 54–71.

Schumpeter, J. A. (1954). *History of Economic Analysis*. New York: Oxford University Press.

Walras, Léon (1874). *Éléments d'économie politique pure*. Paris & Lausanne. Translated by W. Jaffe: *Elements of Pure Economics*. London: Allen & Unwin, 1954.

Part III
The linear market model

1 INTRODUCTION

The topic to be pursued now belongs to the framework reported in Part II, and is a direct continuation of that work. Here we deal with a special case, the *linear market model*, in which the market value functions

$$e_j(p) = p_j S_j(p)$$

are given by

$$e_j = \sum_i p_i a_{ij}$$

for some constant a_{ij}, and so are the elements of the vector e having the linear form

$$e = pa,$$

where a is a constant matrix, the *structure matrix* for the market.

For such a model Walras' Law, generally requiring $eI = 0$ for all p, therefore, requires $paI = 0$ for all p, and hence that

$$aI = 0.[1]$$

Accordingly, by virtue of Walras' Law, the elements in the rows of the market structure matrix all sum to 0.

The price existence question is now whether $p > 0$ exists for which $pa = 0$. For, with $p > 0$, $e = 0$ is equivalent to $S = 0$. The question is considered in the following, where it is approached by a method that shows at the same time how such prices can be arrived at following the Law of Supply and Demand, like the *tâtonnement* of Walras.

---

1 As before in Part II, Appendix III, I denotes a column vector with elements all 1.

2   EXISTENCE QUESTION

With this model, because

$$p_j S_j = e_j$$

$$= \sum_i p_i a_{ij}$$

$$= p_j a_{jj} + \sum_{i \neq j} p_j a_{ij}$$

we have

$$S_j = a_{jj} + \sum_{i \neq j} p_i a_{ij}/p_j,$$

so a_{jj} *is the supply capacity limit for good j in the economy*, approached asymptotically as $p_j \to \infty$. This also holds when prices are restricted to be normalized and $p_j \to 1$, the ratios of other prices being fixed while normalization is preserved. It appears, therefore, that *for a linear market the finite supply capacity condition holds automatically*.

The intercept condition, which requires $e_j < 0$ if $p_j = 0$, now requires

$$\sum_{i \neq j} p_i a_{ij} < 0 \quad \text{for all } p_j \ (i \neq j),$$

so it is equivalent to

$$a_{ij} < 0 \quad (i \neq j).$$

But the slope condition, which is that e_j be decreasing in p_i $(i \neq j)$, is also equivalent to this. Thus, *for the linear market model, the slope and intercept conditions are equivalent*. With Walras' Law, *they both imply*

$$a > 0 \quad \text{for all } j,$$

that is, *positive supply limit for every good*.

The units for goods are at present arbitrary. When $u > 0$ present units of good j are made the new unit, the price p becomes $p_j u_j$, and the excess supply quantity S_j becomes S_j/u_j, so *the excess supply value* $e_j = p_j S_j$ *is unaltered*. With the new units, the elements a_j of the matrix a are replaced by a_j/u; in particular, a_{jj} is replaced by a_{jj}/u_j. Since $a_{jj} > 0$, we can take $u_j = a_{jj}$ and so choose new units to make $a_{jj} = 1$.

It can be understood now that the system has been normalized by this choice of units to make $a_{jj} = 1$ for all j. That is, for any good, *the supply capacity limit has been made the unit of amount*.

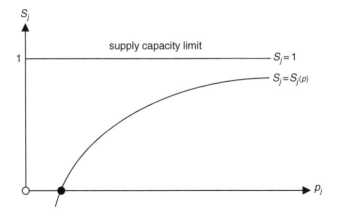

Figure 1 Excess supply curve for good j, prices of other goods being fixed.

For any p_i $(i \neq j)$, the excess supply curve for good j is a rectangular hyperbola with the lines $p_j = 0$ and $S_j = 1$ as asymptotes (see Figure 1). The curve cuts the line $S_j = 0$ where

$$p_j = -\sum_{\neq j} pa_j$$

$$= p_j - \sum p_j a_j$$

$$= \sum p_j b_j,$$

the coefficients b_{ij} being given by

$$b_{ij} = -a_{ij} > 0 \quad (i \neq j),$$
$$b_{jj} = 1 - a_{jj} = 1 - 1 = 0,$$

so that

$$b = 1 - a \geq 0.$$

The condition for $S_j = 0$ for all j is therefore

$$p = pb.$$

Since Walras' Law requires $al = 0$, we have $bI = I$. Thus b, being such that $b > 0$ and $bI = I$, *is a square row distribution matrix*, or a transition matrix as in a Markov process. Because $b_{ij} > 0$ $(i \neq j)$, *it is irreducible*, and so, by the equilibrium theorem for Markov processes shown here in the Appendix, *there exists a unique normalized price vector p for which $p = pb$, and for this,* moreover, $p > 0$. That is, there exist prices p_j, with ratios uniquely determined and all positive, for which $e_j = p_j S_j = 0$ for all j. Since $p_j > 0$, this is equivalent to $S_j = 0$ for all j, as required.

3   *TÂTONNEMENT*

From the theory of distribution matrices, with b irreducible, we not only have the existence of a unique and positive normalized price vector $\bar{p}$ for which $\bar{p} = \bar{p}b$; we also know that it can be found, starting with any initial p, by repeatedly replacing p by pb. That is,

$$pb^t \to \bar{p} \quad (t \to \infty),$$

whatever the initial p.

   An explanation of this process, where p is adjusted each time to pb, is that, given any prices p for all the goods, *the price of each good is altered to exactly the price that would clear its market were all the other prices to remain unaltered.* The other prices do not remain the same, but all are readjusted by the same principle simultaneously, and so none come out quite as intended. But, with the indefinite repetition of the process, there is a convergence to the right prices which clear all markets simultaneously.

   This might be a fair model for the process of arriving at $\bar{p}$, were there some agency in the economy for its realization; in any case, a knowledge of the matrix b would be essential. We have no idea of such an agency, with that kind of knowledge, and this is not the sort of thing to be entertained for the automatic self-regulation of the market.

   Excess supply or demand is known not by a fixed identifiable individual or agency, but in a scattered decentralized way, as soon as a buyer of a good cannot find a seller or a seller a buyer at the price of the last transaction. That price then is no longer the price. The possible price rises or falls, in the minds and readiness of unfulfilled buyers or sellers in the one case or the other, until a transaction takes place, when it becomes the actual price; and so forth. A consistency with this picture is required; it is not exactly the *tâtonnement* of Walras, but more or less the same – and there is no need for the usual auctioneer.

   The adjustment model to be considered, where old current prices p_j become replaced by new prices p_j^* is stated by

$$p_j^* = p_j - v_j e_j,$$

where the $v_j > 0$ are reaction coefficients, or *adjustment velocities*.

For a restatement of this process, we have $r^* = rc$, where

$$r_j = p_j/v_j$$

and

$$c_{ij} = v_i a_{ij} \geq 0 \quad (i \neq j),$$
$$c_{jj} = 1 - v_j a_{jj} = 1 - v_j.$$

Thus $cI = I$, since $aI = 0$. Also, $c \geq 0$ provided $v_j \leq 1$ for all j. In that case c is a distribution matrix, and so, as before, starting with any p, and corresponding r, indefinite repetition of the adjustment produces a convergence, with limit $\bar{r}$ for which $\bar{r} = \bar{r}c$, that is, $\bar{p}^* = \bar{p}$, equivalently $e(\bar{p}) = 0$, or equivalently $S(\bar{p}) = 0$.

The velocities must be positive, to produce an alteration in the prices. They also cannot be so large as to make any price become negative. Over-reaction can be expected anyway to lead not to an eventual settled state, but to produce endless turmoil in the prices; to produce not a final order, but a perpetual chaos. With our particular normalization, involving a choice of units, the requirement for an orderly convergence takes the form

$$0 < v_j \leq 1 \quad \text{for all } j.$$

This is an entirely satisfactory result, as it stands. We could also allow the v_j to vary freely in time, provided the upper and lower limits as time $\rightarrow \infty$ be positive and less than 1. But then we need a theorem about convergence of infinite products of distribution matrices, instead of the familiar theorem about the convergence of powers.

4 THE HYPERBOX: AN ILLUSTRATION

We now consider an economy with any m goods $i = 1, \ldots, m$ and n traders $j = 1, \ldots, n$. When there are just two of each, the Edgeworth diagram can be referred to (Figure 2). But everything considered for the special case has a counterpart for the general case, without any loss of simplicity; the diagram is lost but all the ideas are maintained, and features emerge that are not well represented in the special case. The issue of reducibility, of some subgroup of traders being independent of the others by having all possessions between them that are related to their own wants, is poorly represented when there are just two traders and two goods. For purposes of illustration the individual utility functions are taken to have the Cobb–Douglas form. This assumption exactly produces the linear market model just now investigated, and so everything there also applies here. A further illustrative feature is provided by the matrix w formed by the exponents in the functions. Since the exponents for any one trader which form a column of this matrix are non-negative and sum to 1, each column is a distribution vector, so making this an $m \times n$ rectangular distribution matrix. It is the *want matrix* for the

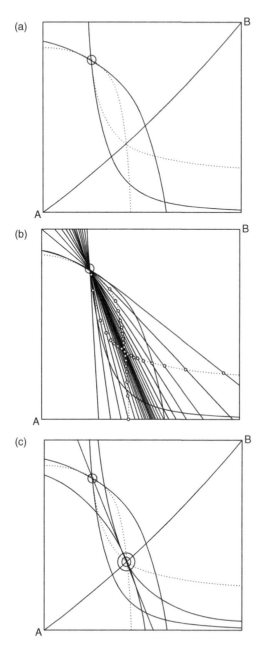

Figure 2 Lessons in Edgeworth's box.
(a) Offer curves, (b) *Tâtonnement*, (c) General equilibrium.

system, its elements expressing the relative weight or intensity with which any trader wants any good. It is such that

$$w \geq 0, \qquad Jw = J,$$

where J is a row vector of any order whose elements are all 1.

We have to deal with the demand behaviour associated with a Cobb–Douglas utility

$$u(x) = A \prod_i x_i^{w_i},$$

where

$$w_i \geq 0, \qquad \sum_i w_i = 1,$$

so the exponents describe a distribution. With a budget constraint $px = M$, the derived demand function is the solution $x = F(p, M)$ for the optimization problem

$$\max u(x): px = M$$

given by

$$x_i = M w_i / p_i.$$

In other words, the expenditure on good i is the share $M w_i$ of the total expenditure M, so this divided by the price gives the quantity of the good demanded.

The n traders in the hyperbox can now be taken to have utility functions

$$u_j(x_j) = A_j \prod_i x_{ij}^{w_{ij}},$$

where

$$w_{ij} \geq 0, \qquad \sum_i w_{ij} = 1,$$

so these exponents form the columns of a rectangular $m \times n$ distribution matrix w.

Another similar rectangular distribution matrix that is involved is the *endowment matrix a*. This is a point in the hyperbox which is the generalized counterpart of Edgeworth's box whose rows tell us how the goods in the economy are distributed to the traders. This is such that

$$a \geq 0, \qquad aI = I,$$

where I is like the vector J but a column vector instead. The two rectangular distribution matrices a and w, one with distributions by rows and the other by columns, give all the parameters for the generalized Edgeworth box economy being considered. The product aw' of one distribution matrix with the transpose of the other is a square distribution matrix, like the transition probability matrix of a Markov process. These distribution matrices have nothing to do with probability, but theorems available from probability theory can be applied to obtain required results. Reducibility of aw' in the sense usually applied to a stochastic matrix, the matrix of transition probabilities in a Markov process, is equivalent to a similar reducibility which applies to the pair a and w simultaneously and has a direct economic sense. The *irreducibility* of aw' or of the pair a, w in the equivalent sense *is necessary and sufficient for positive equilibrium prices to exist, and for these to be unique*. Irreducibility is also the condition for the global convergence of the *tâtonnement* process for finding them, dealt with in this and the last chapters.

Prices are given by a row vector p, and $pI = I$ tells us that they are normalized prices with sum 1. With the allocation a trader j has a bundle of goods a_j from column j, with a value $M_j = pa_j$ which is the income for determining the trader's budget constraint. The column vector M with these elements has transpose $M' = pa$. Because, with normalized prices,

$$M'I = (pa)I = p(aI) = pI = I,$$

the elements sum to 1 so this is a distribution vector, telling us the *income distribution* of traders which is associated with the distribution of goods a and prices p. The demand for good i by trader j is

$$x_{ij} = w_{ij} M_j / p_i,$$

and the supply is a_{ij}, so the excess supply is $a_{ij} - x_{ij}$. The aggregate excess supply for good i is, therefore,

$$S_i = \sum_i \left(a_{ij} - w_{ij} M_j / p_i \right),$$

and so, since $\sum_j a_{ij} = 1$, the excess supply value $e_i = p_i S_i$ is given by

$$e_j = p_i - \sum_i w_{ij} \sum_k p_k a_{kj},$$

that is,

$$e = pb, \quad \text{where } b = 1 - aw'.$$

Because

$$(aw')I = a(w'I) = aI = I,$$

Walras' law, stated by the identity

$$e(p)I = 0, \quad \text{for all } p,$$

is verified. Also if $p_i = 1$, so that $p_j = 0$ $(j \neq i)$ because of price normalization, then $S_i = 1$, so the supply capacity limit of every good is 1.

Thus we have normalized linear market functions of the last section with coefficients $b = 1 - aw'$. Everything said there can apply now, including what was said about the existence and uniqueness of equilibrium prices $\bar{p}$ making $S(\bar{p}) = 0$, about the *tâtonnement* process and the reaction coefficients v, and about the role of irreducibility in all that.

Equilibrium prices p are such that $p = paw'$, and are associated with an income distribution M by the relations $M' = pa$, $p' = wM$ which also give $M = a'wM$. After solving for p, M is determined. Alternatively, one could solve for M in this last relation and then determine p.

5   REDUCIBILITY

Now it will be seen what the irreducibility condition of Section 3 signifies in terms of the allocation and want matrices a and w, which describe the economy. A subgroup T of traders constitute an *independent sub-economy* if the traders between them own all the goods they want. For a statement of that,

$$(j \in T, w_{ij} > 0) \Rightarrow (a_i > 0 \Rightarrow k \in T)$$

in other words, *if trader j is in the group and wants good i, then any trader k who has some of good i must be in the group*. The traders in the group will have no dealings with those outside it since they want nothing the outsiders have. However, those in the group might have things the others want. The economy is *reducible* if such an independent sub-economy exists, and otherwise is *irreducible*. We have to connect this economic sense of reducibility, which applies to a pair of rectangular distribution matrices, with the reducibility condition that familiarly applies to a single square distribution matrix.

With S as the complement of T, the considered condition is equivalent to

$$(j \in T, k \in S) \Rightarrow (w_{ij} > 0 \Rightarrow a_i = 0).$$

Because the terms are non-negative, the right side here is equivalent to

$$w_{ij}a_{ij} = 0 \quad \text{for all } i,$$

and because a sum of non-negative terms is zero if and only if each term is zero this is equivalent to

$$(w'a)_{jk} = \sum_i w_{ij}a_{ik} = 0.$$

The condition, therefore, is

$$(j \in T, k \in S) \Rightarrow (a'w)_{kj} = 0,$$

showing a reduction of the square matrix $w'a$ in the usual sense.

The reduction condition has been stated with reference to a group of traders, but it can also be expressed in terms of a group of goods. Consider a group G of goods owned entirely by traders who want no others, that is

$$(i \in G, a_{ij} > 0) \Rightarrow (w_{kj} > 0 \Rightarrow k \in G),$$

and equivalently, with H the complement of G,

$$(i \in G, k \in H) \Rightarrow (aw')_{ik} = 0,$$

showing a reduction of aw'. Given the first condition on a group T of traders one can form the group

$$G = \{i\colon w_{ij} > 0, j \in T\}$$

of all goods that are wanted by any of them. Also, given the second condition in terms of a group G of goods,

$$T = \{j\colon a_{ij} > 0, i \in G\}$$

is the set of all traders who own any of them. Then the one condition in terms of one group is equivalent to the other condition in terms of the other, and to the condition stated for the matrix $w'a$ and to that for the matrix aw'. In other words a and w having the form

$$a = \begin{bmatrix} & T & \\ G & \cdot & O \\ & \cdot & \cdot \end{bmatrix}, \quad w = \begin{bmatrix} & T & \\ G & \cdot & \cdot \\ & O & \cdot \end{bmatrix}$$

is equivalent to $a'w$ having the form

$$a'w = \begin{bmatrix} & T & \\ T & \cdot & \cdot \\ & O & \cdot \end{bmatrix}$$

and to aw' having the form

$$aw' = \begin{bmatrix} & G & \\ G & \cdot & O \\ & \cdot & \cdot \end{bmatrix}$$

Because a and w are distribution matrices, a by rows and w by columns, so are aw' and $a'w$, by rows and columns, respectively, and these moreover are square. Theorems from the theory of Markov processes can therefore apply to $a'w$ and aw' the irreducibility condition of that theory, applying usually to the matrix of transition probabilities, is now translated into the economic irreducibility condition stated directly in terms of the allocation and want matrices a and w.

Appendix

DISTRIBUTION MATRICES, AGAIN

1   Introduction

Non-negative numbers that sum to 1 describe a distribution of some kind. It could be a distribution of probability, or of good things at a party, or of goods in an economy, as here. A *distribution vector* being one whose elements describe a distribution, a row vector p is a distribution if $p \geq 0$ and $pI = I$, where I is a column vector with elements all 1. A *distribution matrix* is one whose rows, or alternatively columns, are all distribution vectors (Figure 3). Often we have a rectangular distribution matrix since the number of goods is not necessarily the number of sectors in which they are distributed. In this section we deal with a square row-distribution matrix. With a Markov process the distribution matrix involved is formed by the transition probabilities, and is square. The original interest of distribution matrices derives from this context, and so does the theory. In such a probability context they are called stochastic matrices. By a *transition matrix* here we can mean a square distribution matrix, free of the probabilistic connection.

For a typical Markov process, individuals in a population have n possible states, and from one period to the next an individual in state i will make a transition to state j with probability a_{ij}, so that

$$a_{ij} \geq 0, \quad \sum_j a_{ij} = 1 \qquad \text{for all } i.$$

Of p_i individuals in state i, in one period, $p_i a_{ij}$ will be in state j in the next, so $\sum_i p_i a_{ij}$ will be the total going into state j. Thus, if p is the distribution of individuals over states in one period, then in the next it will be pa. An *equilibrium distribution* is one that is preserved period after period. Thus, for $\bar{p}$ to be an equilibrium, it should be a distribution vector such that $\bar{p}a = \bar{p}$. Main theorems about transition matrices concern the existence and stability of an equilibrium. This is just like in the theory of general economic equilibrium. In fact, such theorems have an application there, as was shown in this chapter and the last. For another, quite different topic, in dealing with Sraffa's prices, in addition to the existence question that arises, the stability of an adjustment process is settled by the same means. Shortage or surpluses of value going to sectors in one period, because the prices are not correct, are compensated by price adjustments in the next. Each price is adjusted regardless of the adjustments of the others, as if they were to remain the same. But the others also are adjusted, so each must be readjusted endlessly, but there is a convergence. This is quite like the Walrasian *tâtonnement*; in a special case, each price is adjusted so as to clear its own market were the other prices to remain fixed, but they also are adjusted, and so forth. But still, Sraffa's prices have nothing to do with the equilibrium of supply and demand, since in this model these are fixed and unalterable. Both orders of ideas now have an equitable share in equilibrium and stability.

In studies about general equilibrium in a Cobb–Douglas world, found in this chapter, again we have distribution matrices, though in this case they are not square but rectangular. Many goods are distributed to many individuals, and weights associated with the wants of the individuals are distributed over the goods. Though the two distribution matrices so obtained are rectangular, they multiply together to give a square one to which available theorems apply, with implications for the existence and stability of positive equilibrium prices. Arguments applied to distribution matrices also have useful applications in the Leontief input–output model, and more generally in the von Neumann model. Irreducibility conditions familiar from the theory of Markov processes translate into the (welcomed or not) one-interdependent-world situation envisaged in economics, with consequences for prices instead of probabilities.

For a greatly simplified and satisfactory theory of markets, we have our linear model, which still gives a full representation of the main questions; and, instead of apparatus from topology and differential equations, there is a dependence on nothing more elaborate than the finite algebra of distribution matrices. Even when we drop the linearity, distribution matrices show up again, in dealing with global stability of a flexible type of adjustment process that obeys the Law of Supply and Demand.

2   Existence

The distributions on n objects describe the $(n-1)$-simplex

$$\Delta = \{p\colon pI = 1,\, p \geq 0\}.$$

The indices $1, \ldots, n$ are labels for its vertices, and subsets of vertices specify the faces. For another description, the simplex is the locus of centroids when a unit mass is distributed to its vertices. Each vertex becomes the centroid or centre of gravity when the entire mass is concentrated on it, and a face is described when the mass is concentrated on a subset of vertices. When negative weights are permitted, we have the barycentric coordinates familiar in analytic geometry, which sum to 1, with a triangle and, more generally, a simplex of references. The effect of the non-negativity restriction is to confine points to the region given by the simplex itself, instead of having them range in the carrier space of the simplex.

A distribution matrix a can be regarded as a mapping

$$a : \Delta \to \Delta$$

of the simplex into itself, any point $p \in \Delta$ having an image $pa \in \Delta$. For, given that

$$a \geq 0, \qquad aI = I,$$

if

$$p \geq 0, \qquad pI = 1,$$

so that $p \in \Delta$, and if $q = pa$, then $q \geq 0$ and also

$$qI = (pa)I = p(aI) = pI = 1,$$

so that also $q \in \Delta$. An equilibrium is a fixed point in the mapping, one which coincides with its image, or such that $pa = p$. The following theorem shows the existence of an equilibrium.

Theorem (existence)   If

$$a \geq 0, \qquad aI = I,$$

then $pa = p$ for some p such that

$$p \geq 0, \qquad pI = 1.$$

For proof, there will be use of the following:

Theorem of alternatives   For any matrix a,
either

$$ax = 0 \quad \text{for some } x \gtrsim 0$$

or

$$ua < 0 \quad \text{for some } u$$

and not both.[2]

This proposition is well known and can be submitted now without proof. However, there is a convincing way of looking at it geometrically.

---

2 $x \gtrsim 0$ means $x \geq 0$ and $x \neq 0$.

The convex cone generated by the columns of a is

$$V = \{ax: x \geq 0\},$$

and

$$\Lambda = \{q: q \in V, -q \in V\}$$

is a linear manifold, the *vertex manifold* of V, whose dimension is the *vertex dimension* of V. The cone is *pointed* if its vertex dimension is 0. Assuming no column of a is null, the first possibility in the proposition is that the cone is not pointed. The second possibility is that the columns of a all lie in an open half-space cut by a hyperplane through the origin – geometrically plausible as a necessary and sufficient condition that the cone be pointed.

By this theorem, with $a - 1$ transposed in place of a, either we have the required conclusion in the theorem to be proved, or, alternatively,

$$ax < x \quad \text{for some } x. \tag{i}$$

Therefore, it is enough to show the hypothesis in the theorem excludes this possibility.

Should there be such x as in (i), let $x_r = \min x_i$, so that

$$x_i - x_r \geq 0 \quad \text{for all } i.$$

Then, because $a \geq 0$, we have

$$\sum_i a_{ri}(x_i - x_r) \geq 0. \tag{ii}$$

Also, because $aI = I$, we have $aIx_r = Ix_r$, and so, subtracting this from (i),

$$a(x - Ix_r) < x - Ix_r,$$

which gives, in particular,

$$\sum_i a_{ri}(x_i - x_r) < x_r - x_r = 0,$$

contradicting (ii) and so denying (i).   ☐

3 Uniqueness

A subset v of the vertices $1, \ldots, n$ specifies a face Δ_v of the distribution simplex Δ, so if w is the complementary subset, then

$$p \in \Delta_v \Leftrightarrow p_j = 0 \quad \text{for all } j \in w.$$

The distribution matrix a is *reducible* Δ_v if $\Delta_v a \subset \Delta_v$, that is, if

$$p \in \Delta_v \Rightarrow pa \in \Delta_v,$$

or the image of every point in Δ_v is also in Δ_v. In this case, we have

$$\sum_{i \in v} p_i a_{ij} = 0 \quad \text{for } j \in w.$$

Since a sum of non-negative terms is zero if and only if each term is zero, this is equivalent to

$$p_i a_{ij} = 0 \quad \text{for } i \in v, j \in w$$

and this, being true for all $p \in \Delta_v$, is equivalent to

$$a_{ij} = 0 \quad \text{for } i \in v, j \in w.$$

Reducibility of a therefore means the existence of a subset v of vertices, with complement w, for which this is true.

The term applies similarly to a Leontief input–output matrix where there is an independent subgroup of sectors, whose required inputs are supplied entirely by their own outputs. Some arguments about a Markov transition matrix apply just as well to a Leontief matrix.

Theorem (uniqueness)   For a transition matrix a with an equilibrium p, in order that $p > 0$ it is necessary and sufficient that a be irreducible, and then and only then is the equilibrium p unique.

Let $v = \{j: p_j > 0\}$, so that v is non-empty, since $p \geq 0$, and $pI = 1$, and the complement w being non-empty denies $p > 0$. Then, since $p = pa$, we have

$$\sum_{i \in v} p_i a_{ij} = 0 \quad (j \in w).$$

Since $p_i a_{ij} \geq 0$ this is equivalent to

$$p_i a_{ij} = 0 \quad (i \in v, j \in w),$$

which, since $p_i > 0$ $(i \in v)$, is equivalent to

$$a_{ij} = 0 \quad (i \in v, j \in w).$$

Here we have that a is reducible if w is non-empty. Therefore if a is irreducible w must be empty; that is, $p > 0$. Also if is reducible, say again on the set v, and p

an equilibrium, with

$$\sigma = \sum_{j \in v} p_j$$

$$q_j = (1/\sigma)p_j \quad (j \in v)$$
$$q_j = 0 \qquad\qquad (j \in w),$$

q would be a new equilibrium where $q > 0$ is denied. Therefore, irreducibility is also necessary in order to always have $p > 0$ for an equilibrium.

With irreducibility, the equilibrium p must be unique. For were q another, let

$$t = \min\ p_i/q_i, \qquad r = p - tq,$$

so that $r \geq 0$ while $r_i = 0$ for some i, and also $ra = r$, which, unless $r = 0$, implies reducibility. Hence $r = 0$, that is $p = tq$, which with $pI = 1, qI = 1$ implies $t = 1$ and $p = q$. $\qquad\qquad\Box$

4   Stability

An equilibrium $\bar{p}$ is *stable* if, starting with any p,

$$pa^r \to \bar{p} \quad (r \to \infty).$$

In this case the equilibrium must, moreover, be unique.
Because $\bar{p}a = \bar{p}$, we have $\bar{p}a^r = \bar{p}$, and hence

$$pa^r - \bar{p} = (p - \bar{p})a^r,$$

so stability requires

$$(p - \bar{p})a^r \to 0 \quad (r \to \infty).$$

Now by the theorem of Part II, Appendix III, if μ is the minimum element in some column of a, then

$$\left|(p - \bar{p})a^r\right| \leq |p - \bar{p}|(1 - \mu)^r$$
$$\to 0 \quad \text{if}\quad 0 < \mu < 1.$$

This shows that stability is implied if $\mu > 0$, as may be when a has a positive column.

Theorem (stability)   Any transition matrix with a positive column has a stable equilibrium.

(a)

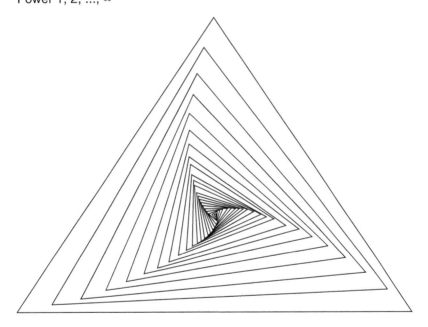

Figure 3a Distribution matrix powers – graphic image.

(b)
```
DATA   Distribution Matrix Powers

'   POWER.BAS
'   Graphics of powers

CLS : KEY OFF: SCREEN 2 : ESC$=CHR$(27)
READ H$: LOCATE 1, 28: PRINT H$;
DEFINT I-K, P, U, X
DIM A(3, 3), B(3, 3), U(3, 1), X(3, 1), T(3)

GOTO BaseSimplex

Check:
 K$ = "": WHILE K$ = "": K$ = INKEY$: WEND
 IF K$ = ESC$ THEN SCREEN 0: KEY ON: END ELSE RETURN

BequalsBA: '_____ B = BA, draw B, repeat
 FOR I = 1  TO 3: FOR J = 1 TO 3: T = 0: FOR K = 1 TO 3
 T = T + B (I, K) * A(K, J): NEXT: T(J) = T: NEXT
 FOR J = 1 TO 3: B(I, J) = T(J): NEXT J, I
 GOSUB Vertices: P = P + 1: LOCATE 3, 1
 PRINT "power"; P;: GOSUB Check: GOTO BequalsBA

Vertices:

 FOR I = 1 TO 3: FOR K = 0 TO 1: X = 0
  FOR J = 1 TO 3:
    X = X + B(I, J) * U(J, K)
  NEXT: X(I, K) = X:
  NEXT K, I
 FOR K = 0 TO 1: X(0, K) = X(3, K): NEXT
 '_____ draw the simplex
 FOR I = 1 TO 3
  LINE (X(I-1, 0), X(I-1, 1))-(X(I, 0), X(I, 1)), 1
 NEXT: RETURN

BaseSimplex:
 FOR I = 1 TO 3: FOR K = 0 TO 1: READ U(I, K): NEXT K, I
 DATA 320,16,80,190,560,190
 '___ which?
 LOCATE 3, 72: INPUT "example", E
 IF E THEN FOR I = 1 TO 9 * E: READ R: NEXT
 '___ read it
 FOR I = 1 TO 3: B(I, I) = 1: FOR J = 1 TO 3
 READ A(I, J): NEXT J, I
 '___ draw the base
 GOSUB Vertices: GOTO BequalsBA
 '_____ examples

 DATA  .1,   .1,    .8,    .1,    .8,   .1,    .8,    .1,    .1
 DATA  .1,   .2,    .7,    .2,    .7,   .1,    .7,    .1,    .2
 DATA  .9,   .075, .025,  .025,  .9,   .075,  .075,  .025,  .9
 DATA  .1,   .1,    .8,    .2,    .7,   .1,    .7,    .1,    .2
 DATA  .1,   .1,    .8,    .6,    .3,   .1,    .05,   .85,   .1
 DATA  0,    .9,    .1,    .1,    0,    .9,    .9,    .1,    0
 DATA  0,    .95,   .05,   .05,   0,    .95,   .95,   .05,   0
```

Figure 3b Distribution matrix powers – BASIC program.

Part IV
Market & Myth

About the idea of an optimum and
its abuses, especially in doctrine
related to the market.

In speech of today a single being, the Market, is at the centre of existence. It is the self-created, self-regulated, unquestioned measure of everything. The textbooks teach that, but for objectionable intrusions, or 'imperfections', its rule would be *optimal*.

It has been remarked that every age has its myth, proclaimed as the higher truth; here we have ours. It permeates every sphere – which could perhaps interfere with visibility. As a movement in the immediate present it is on a gallop with fresh energy, commanding submission everywhere.

In history, this myth, and the reality which would go with it where the human factor is something like an accident, is really rather new. Now it is propagated by endlessly repeated teaching, and bolstered by interests, and inertia. A first impulse for present objections came simply from encounter with the textbook teaching, and being struck by its thorough absurdity and deceptive use of language. This is unaltered by the mathematical dress given to it, and enunciation of portentous theorems. While such presentation may give it all an aura of lofty science and unassailable truth, it is anything but that.

Such a concern might appear simply scholastic, a field of sport for any with the training and inclination and otherwise of no account, like many another. Faults with the teaching have been pointed out many times, but this appears to make no difference. As indoctrination it has a now ominous persistence. With inheritance from the nineteenth century based on inchoate notions from France in the seventeenth we are approaching the twenty-first. Instead of being rudely awakened, as happened lately on another side, it could still be asked whether this is the way to face the now well recognized and already well advanced, developing and encircling realities.

The question requires a regard for the market teaching which has importance from its influence, and apart from that is an exhibition of self-deception – a spectacle to make the power of reason as much of a myth as what it pretends to offer. Of course we know reason has its intermittences; and F. A. Hayek has spoken well about authority in economics and the transmission of mistakes, how they are handed down with uncritical acceptance simply because of the prestige of their perpetrators.

Without the barriers that not long ago always prevailed, when markets were auxiliaries, subordinate to life in a locality, the market dictatorship would most likely impose itself anyway, by its own law, regardless of what anyone should say or think about it. As well accepted, liberty requires a constant defence. Now the absolute rule is fostered by absurd reasoning of scholastics, joined with zealous belief of creatures of the days of innocence which are no longer with us.

We have a concern with the Maximum Doctrine of Perfect Competition which is central to the dominant 'neoclassical' economics. It appears to have originated in the seventeenth century with François Quesnay and the Physiocrats, and was imported from France into the United States by Dupont. For perfect competition there are the well known conditions, and the conclusion – which for the Physiocrats was nothing but self-evident – is that under these conditions the economy achieves an optimum. This is the "social maximum" alluded to by Kenneth J. Arrow in motivating his theory of *Social Choice and Individual Values*:

> If we continue the traditional identification of rationality with a maximization of some sort, then the problem of achieving a social maximum derived from individual desires is precisely the problem which has been central to the field of welfare economics.

What is the criterion by which one can know the better and the worse and hence what is best, or the optimum? Nobody knows. Without a knowledge of this, what we have been told must be quite empty. There could be cause for an abandonment of the whole idea, and surprise at how it is accepted without a tremor by the multitude of the faithful.

To be *free, and yet a good slave* – put that way it sounds ridiculous, though it should strike one the teaching is just like that. First there is the individual freedom in the self-regulated order, the market. Then as if here is not enough to the system, and in further praise of it, it is submitted that the overall result is *efficient*, as an obedient slave performing some precise duty to the utmost. It is a relief one never is told what the duty is. The social objective is taken to exist and to govern because it is talked about. With more known about it there would be a better position to verify whether or not it is at a maximum. For some the loose end is put out of the way as the Aggregation Problem, but should anyone ever get to that problem they would not know what it is.

We are faced with a phenomenon appreciated in another case, the famous "happiness" formula, known as a Marxist slogan though it has an earlier origin. P. P. Wiener attributes it to Frances Hutchison the teacher of Adam Smith. Its classic attribution is to the Utilitarians and Marxists must have borrowed it from them. According to I. Philips:

> John Bowring says in his Deontology [1834, p. 100] that Jeremy Bentham recalled how on a visit to Oxford in 1768 he had first come across the phrase 'the greatest happiness of the greatest number', in Joseph Priestley's Essay on the first principles of Government, published in that year, 1768. "It was from that pamphlet [Bentham said] ... that I drew the phrase, the words and import of which have been so widely diffused over the civilized world. At the

sight of it, I cried out, as it were in an inward ecstasy like Archimedes on the discovery of the fundamental principle of hydrostatics, $E\upsilon\rho\eta\kappa\alpha$."

We should try to find out what the stirring formula could possibly mean. Since "widely diffused" without any qualification, we may look for its import in a simple possible world, one where a cake is distributed over a number n and happiness is the size h of the slice anyone gets. Then the greatest h for the greatest n is wanted. To put all this mathematically, with the size of a slice measured by its angle in radians, so the whole cake is 2π we have the constraint $hn \leq 2\pi$ and have to maximize h and n simultaneously. Let anyone try!

Economics students receive the notion that if no one can have more, unless someone has less, then we have an "optimum". It is tagged with Pareto's name. It is just like with the cake, so apparently you can distribute it around to everyone any way you please, it's always optimal. Good news for the party host as for the economics catechism. Since everyone wants more, this would have to be a case of "Multi-objective Optimization" – the title of a lecture I once saw announced. But there can be no such thing. If you have one objective then you cannot at the same time also have another – you just have to make up your mind!

Impressive absurdities on the same model had occurred previously, for instance Quesnay's Economic Principle "greatest satisfaction with the least labour-pain", and he must have drawn inspiration from Leibniz whose "best of all possible worlds" provided the greatest good at the cost of the least evil. The precedents give a reminder of Hayek's remark about the transmission of mistakes.

Obviously if you choose to maximize one thing, then you cannot at the same time make a free choice of another. You may be lucky, for instance if (x, y) is subject to $x \leq 1$, $y \leq 1$ and you want to simultaneously maximize x and y, this is provided by $(1, 1)$. But we do not have a case like this in dealing with the "happiness" formula, or the cake; for when n is made large h is forced to be small, and *vice versa*.

It may be wondered how anyone, whose respected output is supposed to be rational (in an ordinary sense), can make such remarks, and how they can then have acceptance, even be awarded prizes. On submitting about wrong reasons to Chalongphob Sussangkarn, on a visit with a Thai trade delegation, he gave a healthy answer: "We have the right thing – never mind those reasons!"

Here is another thought bright with free market devotion, from Robert Heilbroner in *The Worldly Philosophers*:

> Edgeworth's pleasure machine assumption bore wonderful intellectual fruit... it could be shown – with all the irrefutability of the differential calculus – that in a world of perfect competition each pleasure machine would achieve the highest amount of pleasure that could be meted out by society.

Enjoyment of the wonderful fruit should in this case be spoilt by a suspicion of worms. What is "all the irrefutability of the differential calculus"? Is it irresistible authority of the Chain Rule; or final truth in the Infinitesimal unphased by digital diversions; or the incomprehension and boredom of all those readers who give a passing glance at the exhibition of machinery and then get on with the text?

We should do that first since the outer skin of this fruit is not without blemishes. We are faced once more with the Leibnizian nonsense, expanded into *n* dimensions. That ought to be a relief since now there should really be no need to go back to that skipped-over calculus after all. However, belief that there is complete relief is feeble *optimism* – a dream of *rationality*. The particular calculus turns up in countless textbooks – at least now we may perhaps know where it started.

For a separate matter where there is a striking inconsistency, something like in the "happiness" formula, Mr James Baker the erstwhile US Secretary of State toured the newly independent republics of Central Asia, speaking with their leaders and submitting what is expected of them: "democratic government and free-market economics". The principle of such government must include some independence. In allowing that, how can it also be laid down what they should decide? A people could wish to maintain competition internally to brace up performance and exploit local capacities, perhaps on the side of basics for people and territory, without putting these at the mercy of a noisy global competition for which they are thoroughly ill-prepared – in other words, settle for living happily with their comparative disadvantage. Instead of doubling their population in thirty years or so they might even choose to limit themselves – and pursue "greatest happiness" for their steady number! After all, if one couple have three children its an appalling 50% expansion in one generation, draining away surplus for improvements, if any. Human rights which get eager attention and have been listed at Helsinki are no doubt good. Nonetheless, it is not always clear where the rights come from, and whether people in a chaotically crowded world have any rights at all. How about obligations, and shouldn't they come first? The signatories of the accord could then form a truly well-considered trading block.

There is a strong tide in favour of knocking down trade barriers and fostering growth, but also a rising opposition coming out of concerns with ecology, resources, demographics, environment and the like, and deteriorations throughout the world. At an earlier time the collision was rather between economic and social factors. Karl Polanyi (1944) gives an account. Now a completely new era has arrived in which hanging over everything are broad questions of survival with a rather short time horizon. Near the threshold of subsistence there are no margins, and with a tight global competition, in a great part divorced from local attachments, there are none either. That covers the most numerous and also the most rich and powerful elements. So where is the will or strength to alter the current course? This is the question dealt with provocatively by Richard Falk in his *Explorations at the Edge of Time*.

J. M. Keynes reviewed the accounts and gave a reconsideration of usual wisdom about trade in his 1933 article on "National self-sufficiency". He was perhaps thinking about other things, but what he had to say may cut better now than it could at that time.

The Earth is not a remote abstraction but a patchwork of localities, each quite immediate to whoever happens to be there. Nor is humanity, which consists of actual people all living somewhere. Besides the currently topical global outlook, if there is a relationship that has priority it is that between people and where they live. The place is a first base for life and sustenance of inhabitants, who are its custodians; all that goes with it is their care and responsibility, and if they make a disaster of it, it is mainly their hardship and their own fault. Such a severe view seems in harmony with remarks of Keynes, and invites consideration as a response to ruinations that take place. In any case, there is unrest in being dependent for vital needs on trade with others with whom no steadier bond exists.

Since every era has something like its own economics, dissatisfaction with what we now have may reflect a transition. But to what? Some say a "new paradigm" without suggestion of its nature or what should be done about it. Propensities in the neoclassical and Marxist phases give visions of another heady round of 'theory'. The neoclassical outlook originated from the time of Newton and the euphoria over his mechanics, and the 'Optimism' of Leibniz. The economy had then to be approached as a machine, not well understood because nobody around had made it or had the plan. Hence the models economists play with, and the cult of the optimum – "the best is enemy of the good" – may be recalled at this point. Marx under the spell of fashionable Hegel took on his notions helplessly, and adopted Ricardo's theory of value without noticing the actual arithmetic is impossible. What could be next? Documentation of happenings to the globe such as State of the World reports of the Worldwatch Institute, or *The Ecologist*, suggest things are going to be different. They cannot be better – let alone *optimal*, if that myth can be dispelled – simply by submitting to government by the self-regulating machine and giving anxious attention to its ups and downs that dominate the news. There must no doubt be withdrawal from that foolishness, though there cannot be a ready-made design for an era with unprecedented features – and touch of finality.

BIBLIOGRAPHY

Afriat, S. N. (1965). People and Population. *World Politics* 17, 3, 431–9. Japanese translation, with foreword by Edwin O. Reischauer: *Japan–America Forum* 11, 10 (October), 1–28.

—— (1972). Reservations about market sovereignty: four notes. In Mundell (1972).

—— (1980). *Demand Functions and the Slutsky Matrix*. Princeton Studies in Mathematical Economics, 7. Princeton: Princeton University Press.

—— (1987a). *Economic Optimism*. Economics Department, Stanford University, 21 April.

—— (1987b). *Logic of Choice and Economic Theory*. Oxford: Clarendon Press.

—— (1988). Optimism from Leibniz to Modern Economics. Sophia University, Tokyo, 27 April.

Afriat, S. N. (1994). On Trade, and Self-sufficiency. Institute of Economics and Management Science, Kobe University, 22 April 1988. *Research Paper* No. 326 (April 1989), School of Economic and Financial Studies, Macquarie University, New South Wales.

Arrow, K. J. (1951). *Social Choice and Individual Values*. New York: John Wiley. 2nd edition 1963.

Brecher, Irving and Donald J. Savoie (Eds) (1993). *Equity and Efficiency in Economic Development: Symposium in Honour of Benjamin Higgins*. Montreal: McGill-Queen's University Press.

Bell, Daniel and Irving Kristol (1982). *The Crisis in Economic Theory*. New York: Basic Books.

Braudel, Fernand (1981). *Civilization and Capitalism*. New York: Harper and Rowe.

Cassidy, John (1996). The Decline of Economics. *The New Yorker*, 2, December, pp. 50–60.

Deane, Phyllis (1978). *The Evolution of Economic Ideas*. Cambridge: Cambridge University Press.

Falk, Richard (1992). *Explorations at the Edge of Time: The Prospects for World Order*. Tokyo: United Nations University Press and Philadelphia: Temple University Press.

Goldsmith, Edward (1992). *The Way: An Ecological World View*. London: Rider.

Hansen, Bent and Girgis A. Marzouk (1965). *Development and Economic Policy in the UAR (Egypt)*. Amsterdam: North-Holland.

Hayek, F. A. (1974). The Pretence of Knowledge. Nobel Memorial Lecture, Stockholm, 11 December. In Hayek (1978), Chapter 2.

—— (1978). *New Studies in Philosophy, Politics, Economics and the History of Ideas*. Chicago: University of Chicago: Press.

Heilbroner, Robert (1972). *The Worldly Philosophers*. New York: Simon and Schuster.

Higgins, Benjamin (1989). Equity and efficiency in development: basic concepts. In Brecher and Savoie (1992), Chapter 1.

Hutchison, T. W. (1977). *Knowledge and Ignorance in Economics*. Chicago: University of Chicago Press.

Keynes, J. M. (1933). National Self-sufficiency. *The New Statesman and Nation*, 8 and 15 July; *The Yale Review*, Summer; *Collected Writings* D. Moggridge (Ed.) London: Macmillan (1982), Vol. XXI, 233–46.

Leijonhufvud, Axel (1968). *Keynesian Economics and the Economics of Keynes*. New York: Oxford University Press.

—— (1973). Life among the Econ. *Western Economic Journal* 11, 3 (September).

Morowitz, Harold (1981). Entropy, a New World View by Jeremy Rivkin and Ted Howland. *Discover*, January, 83–5.

Mundell, R. A. (Ed.) (1972). *Policy Formation in an Open Economy*. Proceedings of the Conference at the University of Waterloo. Waterloo, Ontario: Waterloo Research Institute.

Polanyi, Karl (1944). *The Great Transformation: the Political and Economic Origins of Our Time*. New York: Rinehart & Co. Inc. (and Boston: Beacon Press, 1957).

Samuelson, Paul A. (1970). Maximum Principles in Analytical Economics. Nobel Memorial Lecture, Stockholm, 11 December. In *Les Prix Nobel en 1970*. Amsterdam and New York: Elsevier.

Shubik, Martin (1970). A Curmudgeon's guide to microeconomics. *Journal of Economic Literature* 18, 2.

Soros, George (1997). The Capitalist Threat. *The Atlantic Monthly*, February, 45–58.

Symons, Michael (1987). In Adelaide, the Collapse of the Free Market. Sydney, NSW: *Times on Sunday*, 3 May, p. 35.

Tarascio, Vincent J. (1986). The crisis in economic theory: a sociological perspective. *Research in the History of Economic Thought and Methodology* 4, 283–95.
Ukai, Yasuharu (1987). Cycles of Isolationism and Foreign Trade – a case study of Japan. *Kansai University Review of Economics and Business* 16, 1 (September), 61–74.
Worldwatch Institute (2000). *State of the World 2000.* New York and London: W. W. Norton & Co.

Part V
On trade, and self-sufficiency

Walk ever in the path of truth – with a sneer

Voltaire to d'Alembert

1 An introduction to economics

I welcome this opportunity to pay tribute to Benjamin Higgins.[1] Because I have a regard for Ben the individual as well as the economist, a few recollections will not be out of place, and they provide a setting for what I submit on questions the two of us sometimes tried to discuss.

Our paths have crossed at various times since the 1960s. We first met when he was at the University of Texas in Austin and I was at Rice University, Houston. Then in Ottawa I joined him as a colleague. His retirement – not the suitable word, nor is 'advancement' though 'advance' might do – was a loss. He went to Australia, homeland of his wife Jean Higgins.

Our meetings did not so much involve talk of economics as conviviality. When we did get to economics the recurrent theme was, as it is now, that something was wrong. Aware of our differences in focus and failure of language, we never got anywhere and left the subject, only to return. Perhaps it was our disposition as writers instead of readers or listeners that impeded communication. This present occasion is a chance to bridge the gap.

Visiting Australia in 1987, I spent my first weekend at the Higgins's 'Post' (a thousand acres, some sheep). After a misadventure with the train from Canberra, Jean Higgins turned up in Cooma to drive us to Kallarroo. In that incredible isolation, before a blazing fire fed from gum trees that, because of compensating drafts, in fact did little to warm the Post, the old subject came up again.

For Thomas Malthus it may have been "the dismal science" but of course economics is not free of strong feelings nor even quite a science. For lack of a common bedrock positions are governed by variable opinion, tradition, pressure, personal belief or interest, or some respected "scribbler". An amount of heat goes into whether markets should be 'free' or not. Credibility is a constant issue – present company not excepted.

Graeme Dorrance from the Australian National University was among the group assembled there. He said, with quiet confidence of settled belief, that it was odd

---

1 Symposium on *Equity and Efficiency in Economic Development* in Honour of Benjamin Higgins, Canadian Institute for Research on Regional Development, University of Moncton, New Brunswick, 1991.

to have complaint from one such as myself, a typical embodiment of what was wrong with the profession. My association is with mathematical economics and he shared the idea that salvation would come only when such diversions are put aside, to allow a genuine concern with real issues.

I would respond by saying that closeness to issues may give relevance and weight, and a good conscience, but must be a distraction. As it was with another doctrine lately, so it is with economic teaching: while certain things may have important influence they are nevertheless misleading, maybe an abuse of mind and language. Should economists have a concern with such issues? In the main, the profession continues confidently and regardless, with little self-examination. Government of the group decides the games to play, and the "Crisis in Economic Theory" which has been so much discussed lately is just a tantrum in the Toy Department.

An interesting line to pursue in trying to understand something of the sort that may be wrong is the "Optimism" associated with the idea that trade is connected with a "social maximum" – whatever that may mean. If this were excluded from belief some usual pieties about trade would not look so good and one might even turn to common sense.

At the World Congress of the Econometric Society in Cambridge, UK, after he had won the Nobel Memorial Prize, Paul Samuelson confessed his motivation: "adulation of the economics profession". As much as reality to do with economy also the profession itself is worthy of study. We already have Axel Leijonhufvud's classic on the model of Gulliver.[2] Another contribution comes from Robert Kuttner.[3] At the start Kuttner says "Events have been unkind to the economy, and unkinder still to economists", and "Since 1970 an outpouring of serious and ideologically diverse articles and books has pronounced that economics is in a state of severe, perhaps terminal, crisis". There seems to be a sharper focus on life of the profession but "the ship sails on" and what difference will it make? [4] Thomas Malthus was worried about abuse of language in his *Definitions in Political Economy* (1827) and he would not be happier now.

Clearing decks helps with management of disorder and creates space. Certainly the "optimism" should be given up and the wilderness that results would have to be an improvement.

When a distinguished practical capitalist can express in public his reservations about "free-market" culture, it makes news.[5] For now we have from George Soros:[6] "Although I have made a fortune in the financial markets, I now fear that the untrammelled intensification of laissez-faire capitalism and the spread of market values into all areas of life is endangering our open and democratic society. The main

2 Life among the Econ, *Western Economic Journal* 11, 3 September 1973. Reprinted in Dimand (1986).
3 The Poverty of Economics: A Report on a Discipline Riven with Epistemological Doubt on the One Hand and Rigid Formalism on the Other, *Atlantic Monthly*, February 1985.
4 The Decline of Economics, *New Yorker*, 2 December, 1996, pp. 50–60.
5 Eric Ipsen, Capitalism's King Spies Evil in Market-Mad Realm. *International Herald Tribune*, 16 January, 1997, pp. 1 and 6.
6 The Capitalist Threat. *Atlantic Monthly*, February 1997, pp. 45–58.

enemy of the open society, I believe, is no longer the communist but the capitalist threat". But where is – or was, when it was first heard about – the "open society"?

Abandonment of structures leads back towards a primitive level, even to Aristotle. As a complement to Keynes,[7] Aristotle's views about trade and self-sufficiency are impressive. He requires that trade be in the service of self-sufficiency and should not go further (*Politics*, Book I). Adam Smith notwith-standing, the meaning of this idea must be as worthy of study now as it was then.

No one can dispute that trade is basic to economic life even when absurdities about its merits are put aside. At the same time there is no simple notion of what should be meant by self-sufficiency. Opposing views come forward in times of change, so it should not be surprising to hear in a given moment that "In this day and age, there is no such thing as economic self-sufficiency" (Henri de Villiers quoted in *Time*, 27 March, 1989, p. 42) and "There's no longer any such thing as state sovereignty" (Allan Gotlieb quoted in *Ottawa Magazine*, March 1989, p. 22). Ages do pass and this one may do so as promptly as those of recent memory when it was confidently assumed the Affluent Society was here to stay, or that communism would take over. Another has arrived already when the Earth, the general source of maintenance, has maintenance problems itself.

Conflicts between major powers must in some manner be receding, survivors becoming less unlikely. Size serves power, but there could still be a yielding to the smaller groups clamouring for separation. These peoples can then properly look after themselves, stimulated by the immediacy of effects of self-management, on a scale where damage would be more local than global. Maintenance of the Earth may then be more generously forthcoming, since coercion that springs from directly felt self-interest is the most acceptable kind and most to be trusted.

In any case, there might be room for speculations over what remains but none over the part under the "optimism" heading, related as it is to the inchoate intellectual fumblings of early days that persist in the textbooks and minds of well-trained economists. Unburdened of such futilities there is more room to expand, even to arrive – if anyone should insist on some outright simple concept of 'self-sufficiency' – at an absurdity, just the obverse of the one we left.

Kenneth Boulding was able to touch on "The Legitimation of the Market"[8] but legitimacy for the pervasive common-sense practice of economic protection is less readily granted. It is kept that way by what amounts to a metaphysical belief, that an overriding objective should be to knock down barriers to trade to allow domination of a global competition serving an unknown end. Instead of this determination, another objective has been coming forward, one that gives another dimension to efficiency and seems to have more to do with cooperation than competition, namely, the objective of survival.

7 J. M. Keynes, National Self-Sufficiency, *New Statesman and Nation*, 8 and 15 July 1933; *Yale Review*, Summer 1933; Collected Writings Vol. XXI, 233–46. I am indebted to Jim Alvey, of Macquarie University, NSW, for drawing my attention to this paper.
8 Lecture delivered at Rice University, Houston, Texas, 1963.

An efficiency for the market may be granted; there could be a sense to that somewhere though it is certainly not where it is usually put; and in any case markets always spring up when allowed. But such market efficiency could not then be an efficiency as commonly understood. If not just because of the old mistake, perhaps also from a disinclination to capture this sort of efficiency for what it is, economists have come to pick on another efficiency that, to the extent it is in any way understandable, lies altogether in the realm of myth.

The record of failure of development programmes over some decades is frequently noted. Benjamin Higgins, seeking a definition of development, names six proposed definitions and asks "How can reasonable men reach such diverse conclusions"?[9] Another definition may be considered in different ways, both reasonable and unreasonable: the building of self-sufficiency. Such an idea may go against formulas and interests but it has a practical even if shadowy presence. A part of the inclination towards sovereignty is for some form of self-sufficiency. Besides the geographic boundaries, lines are drawn about what is for sale or to be bought, and who are the partners. Inevitably, or for good reason, important capacities are not allowed to atrophy and wither through the exploitation of markets and dependence on vagaries of others.

In regard to economics, and whatever else, with changes taking place a framework is becoming settled where modes of thinking have to be different. Discarding old and taking on new is not a textbook matter such as might be assigned to the care of some accredited professional. Part of the process is liberation from baffled preoccupations of scholastics as well as from absurdities found therein.

Questions about human life have recently come to a new point, where the Earth, once taken for granted as the ready source of all sustenance, has itself become an issue. Aside from the demands of increase of populations, the global economy is a machine for destruction of the Earth itself as well as less earthy inheritance. For a liveable future there has to be an escape from this domination. That this is so is largely left unsaid in declarations about the environment that have been heard everywhere recently.

In the 1960s there was an outbreak of concern about "the population explosion". In 1965 the problem was recognized for the first time at the level of governments, so proponents of population restraint marked that year as the "year of the breakthrough". However, the less-developed countries had this to say: "Make us rich like yourselves and then we will have fewer children". After that the whole matter seemed to disappear underground.

Although public attention has drifted away from the overpopulation issue it remains fundamental. It is commonly thought of as a modern problem noted by Thomas Malthus, but the following gives another idea:

There was a time when numberless races of men wandered the earth. Seeing this Zeus took pity and resolved in the wisdom of his heart to relieve the

9 Equity and Efficiency in Development: Basic Concepts. In Brecher and Savoie (1993), Chapter 1.

all-nourishing Earth of men, stirring up the great quarrel of the Trojan war in
order to lighten the burden by death. The heroes perished in Troy and Zeus'
plan succeeded.

The Cypria, attributed to Stasinos, *c*. 7th–5th century BC

In recent times there has been a speeding up of the exhaustion process that
has been going on for centuries. Fertile regions that once supplied the granaries
in Rome and others exploited by ancient people are now deserts. Vast forests
disappeared simply to supply wood to build those great fleets that used to sail. We
already have an impoverished Earth. In days gone by there was always somewhere
else to spoil. New worlds are no longer so rich, and depredations that formerly
might have taken centuries can now be accomplished quickly.

Destructiveness of warfare has in some way abated, not through any new wisdom
but as a blessing of the Bomb. There is no economic bomb as yet to bring about
a pause; rather, we remain creatures and prisoners of a system that knows only
itself and nothing of its results.

In the 1970s we heard news about "Limits to Growth" supported by computer
printouts and ominous pronouncements from the Club of Rome. It is forgotten
now, a fanciful moment swept away by urgencies of the real business of living:
market competition and growth. The 1980s saw the globalization of markets and
rise of Japan as an economic power. The liberalization of trade and the need to be
competitive in the world market are proclaimed as ruling principles. Surviving in
this economic reality makes an intimidating prospect, even for the powerful.

At the start of the 1990s trading blocks were taking shape, lines being drawn as
though for battle. While a withdrawal from trade may not now be occasion for visit
of a gunboat, multilateral liberalization is dominant, while there are expressions
of concern at signs of a rise in bilateralism, at sovereign parties independently
getting together to serve their own separate interests.

The failure of communism may be a vindication of the market principle, among
other things, but seems to have occurred at a problematic moment for capitalism,
where besides debt there is the many-sided problem related to environment. The
response to this has included measures often to be brought in gradually, or just
studied. For with the preoccupation with competition, and debt, the problem cannot
receive due attention. There is hardly a suggestion that current economic thinking
should change drastically, let alone that it may be destined for anything like the
fate suffered by communism. Even the search for a 'New Economic Order' which
had prominence during the 1960s and 1970s had no manifest outcome.

Many concerned with ecology, environment and population, remain pessimistic,
unsure that a momentum that has grown out of the entirety of past history can
be deflected to deal with an unprecedented and abruptly arrived global problem.
Evidence for looming disaster is ample enough, whether it should issue from
scientific studies or common sense. But such evidence appeals to reason, a poor
teacher and mover to contend with overreaching continuities; another teacher, if
there should be need of one, would be breakdown and calamity.

While markets and trade always remain central to economics, teachings spoil this matter with absurd simplistics and sublime myths inviting the abolition of all barriers – as it were putting everything for sale. There has no doubt been a great trading era, underpinned by devotion to its own myth, the market. One could say: "Never mind wrong reasons, we have the right thing".[10] But those reasons, spurious though they be, have a sufficient durability in minds and textbooks to give sanction to an order that is outliving its welcome.

10 When I submitted these ideas about wrong reasons to Chalongphob Sussangkarn, on a visit with a Thai trade delegation, he replied (I thought very well) with a remark something like this.

2 The 'Optimism' of market doctrine[11]

2.1 CHOICE AND WELFARE

The thread taken up here has connections with 'choice theory' which, being a subject both peculiar and distinct, warrants some separate attention. Choice theory has a certain relevance to development interests and may be associated with efficiency taken broadly. As for equity, F. A. Hayek[12] has provided an interesting view. A similar, though thoroughly antique, notion is 'fair trade'. With all the modern market wisdom, however, fair trade still finds its way into thinking that goes on widely and at every level, though no one quite knows what it means. It seems to be a survivor from early societies, maybe properly active in some situations, where, though it is unspoken, everyone knows what is due to them, or is fair. With trade agreements, however, except where fairness is reflected in some clearly understood reciprocity arrangement, who knows if they are fair or not? Apparently, fairness can only be measured by the degree to which parties honour the agreement, and there certainly can be disputes about that.

Making choices is important for economics – all that could be more important is having the opportunity. But it makes an unresolved subject even where the issues touched are basic. Formal choice theory seems peculiar to economics and it started early. Joseph A. Schumpeter[13] attributes the "Economic Principle", which joins with the idea that the economic problem is a maximum problem, to François Quesnay (1694–1774). It remains permeating the subject as much as ever and a question is whether it overran its proper course. Probably it did that in the beginning and the early words have had a survival.

The accumulation of attention is in proportion to the duration, and though there has been fascinated attention to the works of the clock, still, we are not sure of the time. Matters there are due for settlement, for we have been told "fools rush

---

11 Largely based on my 1987 book *Logic of Choice and Economic Theory*, especially Section I-18 on "The Maximum Doctrine".

12 The Atavism of Social Justice. Ninth R. C. Mills Memorial Lecture, University of Sydney, 6 October 1976. In Hayek (1978), Chapter 5.

13 *History of Economic Analysis*, Oxford University Press, NY 1954.

in where angels fear to tread" and in having that there would be better chance
of company with the latter. The former might make discoveries but that is not
quite what is wanted, though one could be without any and still be far from the
latter. Elaborate structures have been built on precarious drifts of meaning; there
might be a desert without them – but then getting used to it would be much more
economical!

A cause for some general confusion is ambiguity. What is meant by a choice
may be clear, but how, where, or why a choice should be perceived in the first
place may often be less clear. There are problems with terms like 'preference',
'optimum', 'efficient' and 'welfare' for an individual, a group, or an economy.
Often one might wonder whether some proposition is true or false, or neither.
Different organizations or disorganizations of concepts have simultaneous use
and following ordinary usage with key words would be helpful. For example
generalized preferences, without the usual transitivity,[14] are certainly strange;
once it is possible to talk about such things an anchor has gone and anything can
be called anything.

A similar case is the "Pareto optimum". There can be dissatisfaction about
a doctrine that has early origins but still prevails and is represented in the textbooks.
A reading of the "Maximum Doctrine" of the Physiocrats, which is meaningless
taken literally, has been translated into a misreading of Adam Smith's doctrine of
the "Invisible Hand", and this in the hands of mathematical economists using set
language and the like has been translated again, but not very well. In the latest
version we have the Pareto optimum. When that is seen for what it means, in no
ordinary sense is it an optimum: it is just called that while the power it has in
economic thinking is as if it were that. Pareto fleetingly entertained the idea as
being analogous to a maximum and it has come to have exaggerated importance.
It just filled the vacuum created by the shortage of meaning in the old doctrine.

Even if we are assured that Adam Smith did propose a maximality under government by the Invisible Hand – and it is quite possible that he did[15] – we still should
not take the idea seriously. It could be a quaint residue of early thought – after all,
Newton's mechanics is not vitiated by the importance he gave to number magic and
alchemy (perhaps the contrary now, but we can put that aside). It does not matter
what views the Physiocrats or others had about automatic global economic optimization, under various conditions that can be spelt out carefully at length, we still
should not believe in them for we do not and cannot possibly know what they mean.

To the Physiocrats the Maximum Doctrine was not a matter requiring proof – it
was self-evident! There have been gestures to prove it since, out of respect for the
old words mixed with duty to contemporary science, but no one knew quite what
it was that should be proved. Words have patterns both with and apart from their

---

14 If A is better than B, and B is better than C, then (for most) A must be better than C.

15 Tom Settle, Guelph University, has assured me that he did, and provided a copy of the relevant
passage which unfortunately (or fortunately) I have lost. Settle (1976) forcefully expresses a view
similar to the one set out here of the usual textbook teaching.

meaning, as recognized in songs. As interesting as this matter itself is the way it has been preserved, and conditions thinking still. This phenomenon of transmission of authority was pointed out by F. A. Hayek.[16]

2.2   FREE AND YET A GOOD SLAVE – OR OPTIMISM

This title may not be from a well-used stock so that it should tell plainly what it is about, but it suits its purpose. This is pursuit of a thread – that makes embroidery with the optimum, competition, efficiency, welfare and the like – that has run through discourse from early times into the present and latest textbooks. There is an endless repetition and we want to find out what to make of it. If there should be something wrong we would still like to understand whether it is good or not – to know, so to speak, the welfare of it.

What is submitted here has been offered by many writers each in their own way, but this appears to make no difference. How then should one deal with the matter? Perhaps with humour and a look at history. It is not important whether everything reported be right or wrong, as long as things are presented in the right light. For what we have to consider has its own evidence which has nothing to do with history. One may take the clear path of simply looking at the matter itself. But the popularity faced is resistant, and for the reason here the early story may have revelations; in any case, a glance at the salient can come first.

The association of general economic equilibrium, on some model, with a social optimum, or maximum, is paramount in economic teaching. This was the start of welfare economics and related free trade polemics. There can be an approach where everything is reviewed from the ground up, and another, as it were the contrapositive, where we look first at the fruit. The latter is least laborious and enough to raise questions.

To be *free, and yet a good slave* – put that way it seems ridiculous, but it should strike one that the teaching is just like that. First there is the individual freedom, in the self-created, self-regulated stable order, the market. Then as if this were not enough to the system, and in further praise of it, it is submitted that the overall result is efficient, like an obedient slave performing some precise duty to the utmost.

It is a relief that one is never told what the duty is. The social objective is taken to exist and to govern – because it is talked about – and there is discourse on properties of the 'social welfare function' – they are 'revealed'! If more were known about the welfare function we would be in a better position to verify whether or not it is at a maximum. In some minds the loose end is put out of the way by a transfer to the Aggregation Problem, but should anyone ever get to that problem they would not know what it is.

The efficiency entertained in this story is based on the 'commodity space', or some derivative – in its earliest instance quite nebulous and later involving utility.

16 The Pretence of Knowledge. Nobel Memorial Lecture, Stockholm, 11 December 1974. In Hayek (1978) Chapter 2.

The free market may truly have a genuine efficiency, of some sort, but then it would be in another space, not one that has a part in the model. Perhaps it may in some way have to do with taking over the otherwise formidable task of coordinating supply and demand – to encourage some fair allowance for the story, if that were to be an objective.

In one form of the doctrine, competition is central, complex and carefully spelt out at length. In a later form it turns up just as a word, tacked onto statements but doing no work. Here one might puzzle over the real importance of competition and 'competitive equilibrium'. On the other hand, we do recognize the value of competition and its results even if it cannot necessarily be captured in a model. Competition is a stimulus with unheard of results, and having anything unheard of represented in a model amounts to a contradiction in terms.

It takes only two to make a competition more bedrock than perfect competition. There is also useless competition. Competition is ordinarily understood not to be unbridled but to be confined to limited channels; otherwise one may not care for the results, and become exhausted anyway. This may be a complicated subject, unlike the present one which is perfectly simple; perhaps not so simple is the general influence of these ideas.

Contrary to what we read in textbooks, there is not and cannot be a representation of a social optimality in any usual market equilibrium model. This is obvious; however, though something like this has been said many times, it seems not to be acknowledged. Something else not so plain has a stronger influence. Bertrand Russell said "repetition is not a form of argument" but he was speaking maybe as a logician and thinking what we know, that repetition is a form of argument – a powerful one!

2.3 PANGLOSS

A choice has the form of a set with a single element picked out of it. One might question about the distinction of the element – what does it have that the others do not? That it has been chosen and the others have not is impressive: the other points seem to be losers. Then the point is *optimal* – in a sense, which makes the best of all possible worlds of Dr Pangloss, or the optimum of general equilibrium, or the paradox of the "Voting Paradox", or the revealed preference of the bundle of goods bought over all those that might have been bought instead with the same money.

'Optimum' is a term that has a great part in economics, so the sense of it is important. Ordinarily it signifies the best option for a specific purpose, by a criterion related to that purpose. There can be no reservations about that, and adherence to common usage should prevent any different meaning being given to the term, even in some special application. Where a choice is to be made, 'best' means 'chosen', since weighing alternatives as better or worse is only done in order to make a choice between them. There is a way of comparing alternatives, which exists separately in advance of the matter of making a choice and then comes to bear in the choice. Consider, for instance, wanting a heavy stone to serve as an anchor, the heavier the better, and looking around for the best stone, making comparisons. The stones had weight before that need for making a choice arose and regardless of it, and certainly before the optimal stone was found. A disturbing contrast is in 'optimality' cases of economics. An adjustment must be made, and here what is judged to be common usage will be adhered to. There might be an error in the judgement but at least the locus of it will be clear.

Acting so as to achieve the maximum of something has been offered as the definition of rationality. A first question that comes to mind concerns what is actually being said. Does it matter what is being made a maximum? If not then the function that is zero everywhere and thus also a maximum everywhere would serve well. If a strict maximum is wanted, so as to have a full explanation of the uniquely chosen object, a function that is one somewhere and zero elsewhere will be a strict maximum and *optimal* anywhere one wants. Such speculations cannot be part of the meaning of rationality, but still there is no guidance for knowing what is wanted.

Even if we put aside all the problems associated with choice and preference at the individual level, the transfer of the model for an individual to an arbitrary collection of individuals, found in welfare economics, should give us pause. Such a transfer expresses something like the *volontée générale* of the eighteenth century, associated with a collection of individuals being so settled together in some way that it amounted to a unified organism representing an individual of a new order, with a will encompassing all the individual wills. Now we have the same idea, but it involves an arbitrary collection, an abstract set, since nothing is spelt out about the members and their relationship to each other that produces the wonderful result. Modern theories claim to be explicit and to work with models in which everything that is used is always said in advance, if necessary by means of unambiguously stated axioms assisted by a free use of mathematical notations. They never pretended to do that in the rational eighteenth century – in modern dress we have been taken back earlier!

2.4 HISTORICAL

> I have tried to understand what it is that Adam Smith's "invisible hand" is supposed to be maximizing.[17]
>
> Paul Samuelson
> "Maximum Principles in Analytical Economics"

The idea of pursuit of the optimum, the sorting through of possibilities for some purpose to find the best, is understandable and commonplace. But along with it

17 Nobel Memorial Lecture, Stockholm, 11 December 1970. In *Les Prix Nobel en 1970*. Amsterdam and New York: Elsevier. Reprinted in *Science*, 10 September 1971.

are doctrines about an optimum with a global reference produced without any intervention from ourselves. It is taught that a general economic optimum is associated with perfect competition. In another offering – with differences, though they appear not to matter – the optimum belongs to general economic equilibrium, or to a competitive equilibrium, though in this case the competitive seems to do no work and to be simply tacked onto the equilibrium, keeping up appearances in echo of the old doctrine where the competition seems to be important and is spelt out carefully at length. These matters are not in themselves understandable, but how such thinking ever came to be might be found out. That would be useful not only because of the classic cases, but also on account of fallout elsewhere.

A clue is found in historic simultaneity, and other coincidences, with the 'Optimism' of Leibniz. This was ridiculed by Voltaire and is now without influence as such, but it seems to have found a niche in economics where it has been able to survive with better protection. Leibniz, in his *Théodicée* (1710), propounded the doctrine that the actual world is the "best of all possible worlds" chosen by the Creator out of all the possible worlds which were present in his thoughts by the criterion of being the world in which the most good could be obtained at the cost of the least evil. This is the doctrine known as Optimism; in its time it drew a great deal of attention and is famous still. Voltaire's *Candide, ou l'Optimisme* (1759) with the well-known character of Dr Pangloss was "written to refute the system of optimism, which it has done with brilliant success". All this and further information is in the *Oxford English Dictionary*. It was Leibniz who introduced 'optimum' as a technical term on the model of a maximum, and it first came into a dictionary in 1752. We are told:

> The optimism of Leibniz was based on the following trilemma:- If this world be not the best possible, God must either,
>
> 1   not have known how to make a better,
> 2   not have been able,
> 3   not have chosen.
>
> The first proposition contradicts his omniscience, the second his omnipotence, the third his benevolence.

The arguments about the economy are not quite like that. Instead there is a page of calculus, promising infinitesimal precision. It matters not about what, the results are the same. This is a parallel of the Maximum Doctrine that came into economics with François Quesnay and the Physiocrats and flourishes still. It is impressive to find Quesnay's Economic Principle "greatest satisfaction to be attained at the cost of the least labour-pain" perfectly represented in Leibniz's doctrine *vis-à-vis* the Creator's choice criterion. The senseless double optimization, found again with the "greatest happiness of the greatest number" formula, is avoided in the Pareto Optimum. This is not an optimum in the sense intended by Leibniz, even though he abused it, which continues to the present as the understood proper usage. But calling it an optimum shows respect for the old story. Under Pareto Optimism, with regard to the good and evil of the world, there would be the greatest good attainable with the given evil, and the least evil suffered for the good. Begging the main question by a cost–benefit analysis, suitable to mortals who have to get on with the job but no doubt contrary to the law of Heaven, Creation would have been delayed by the need to make a choice between points in the good–evil 'possibility-set' – as we would now say. Leibniz omitted a criterion for that. Were there a marginal price to resolve the matter, with the return of good for evil diminishing to a point of equilibrium, the economic analysis of Creation could have gone further with a use of the new Calculus. There could also have been discourse about the price, the author of it, and why it was not better, or worse.

2.5   ANOTHER REPORT, AND PESSIMISM

By another report, a virus landed on Earth in a meteor and the life that we know emerged through the effort to create a more hospitable environment. The important question then is whether our proper duty is being performed *optimally*. Neglect of the Virus Welfare Function only shows the ignorance that prevails about a fundamental matter.

More on the side of Pessimism, a worry brought forward recently, with a formidable display of erudition in scientific formulae, is Entropy. From Steam Engines, it went into Poetry – and now Economics. It is excellent for poetry, where there is no need for Boltzmann's equation. Now it comes into economics bolstered with all possible equations and a disturbing message: the entropy of the universe is increasing, everything is going downhill, bound to fall apart, final degradation is inevitable, and one is ignorant not to know it. This seems to be the 'Entropy Law' according to the recent innovation in terminology. It confirms the worst suspicions of some ecologists and others about reality, and gives cheer that truth is revealed at last to properly intimidated economists. There has been a stunned silence in the economics profession proper, but a few words by Harold Morowitz, a molecular biochemist of Yale University, serve well as a complete comment.[18]

2.6   IMPORTANT NONSENSE

The impossible 'happiness' formula is now known mostly as a Marxist slogan. But it had an early origin, as does the model for its illogic which came from Leibniz, entered economics with Quesnay, and was accidentally given a new though more subdued life by Pareto, which it still has. P. P. Wiener (1973) attributes the formula to Frances Hutcheson (1694–1746), the teacher of Adam Smith. Its classic attribution is to the Utilitarians, and Marxists must have borrowed it from them.

18 Review of Entropy, a New World View by Jeremy Rivkin and Ted Howland, in *Discover*, January 1981, 83–5.

According to I. Philips:

> John Bowring says in his Deontology [1834, p. 100] that Jeremy Bentham recalled how on a visit to Oxford in 1768 he had first come across the phrase "the greatest happiness of the greatest number", in Joseph Priestley's Essay on the first principles of Government, published in that year, 1768. It was from that pamphlet [Bentham said] that I drew the phrase, the words and import of which have been so widely diffused over the civilized world. At the sight of it, I cried out, as it were in an inward ecstasy like Archimedes on the discovery of the fundamental principle of hydrostatics, $E \upsilon \rho \eta \kappa \alpha$.

Here is another thought, bright with the free market devotion:

> Edgeworth's pleasure machine assumption bore wonderful intellectual fruit it could be shown – with all the irrefutability of the differential calculus – that in a world of perfect competition each pleasure machine would achieve the highest amount of pleasure that could be meted out by society.
>
> Robert Heilbroner, *The Worldly Philosophers* (5th edn, p. 172)

Enjoyment of the wonderful fruit should, in this case, be spoiled by a suspicion of worms. What is all the irrefutability of the differential calculus? Is it like irresistible authority of the Chain Rule? Or final truth in the Infinitesimal, unfazed by digital diversions? Or the incomprehension and boredom of all those readers who give a passing glance at the exhibition of machinery and then get on with the text?

We should do that first, since the outer skin of this fruit is not without blemishes. We are faced once more with the Leibnizian nonsense, expanded into n dimensions. That ought to be a relief, since now there should really be no need to go back to the skipped-over calculus after all. However, belief there is relief is feeble *optimism*, a dream of *rationality*. For the particular calculus turns up in countless textbooks – at least we should know now where it started.

2.7   WELFARE AGAIN

> If we continue the traditional identification of rationality with a maximization of some sort, then the problem of achieving a social maximum derived from individual desires is precisely the problem which has been central to the field of welfare economics.
>
> Kenneth J. Arrow, *Social Choice and Individual Values*, 1951

This statement has influenced a generation, or two, so even if positions have changed in the meanwhile it deserves a comment. For some, possibly everyone, the 'traditional identification' starts here. In any case 'rational' has diverse uses not all to be killed off in the one stroke. Arrow's own use is connected perhaps with another and through carelessness might be taken to be the same. That has to do with the doctrine of free will where man, being endowed with reason, has to choose between good and evil. Man knows good from evil but the choice is still a problem. In welfare economics it is rather the other way round: the determination to choose the best, or maximum, is fully taken for granted; the problem, instead, is knowing the better from the worse. A fair connection might be found if the choice between good and evil were as simple as optimization, but apparently it is not, and dispute is possible. Dr Pangloss was hanged (instead of being burnt – because it was raining!) for speaking about the matter. And poor Candide was beaten just for listening.[19]

The brevity of the above passage conceals a complexity of which this matter of use of a word is only a part. A significance of bringing in rationality at all has to be known. Anything linked with rationality is usually rated a good thing, though the importance of it can be exaggerated. In any case, what is brought before us is something social – never mind what – "derived from individual desires". A sense that can be made out is that the derivation is in some way democratic, with the result for society being decided by its individual members – for instance by taking a vote, though nothing so commonplace is contemplated. One could hold on to this idea as a possibly clear element in the matter. Rescued – or even not – from the quagmire made by company with rationality, maximality, welfare and so forth, it has helped stimulate the attention given to democratic decision processes.

But we should revisit the quagmire. One hears about the 'group mind', though it is difficult to be rational about it, and in any case no one ever said it was rational. The group mind syndrome is manifested in this very subject, and that is how the irrational phenomena in it ought to be understood.

In the 'traditional' adherence, rationality is associated with mind or thought belonging to individuals. However, after maximization has been blessed with the name of rationality by the rhetorical "if then" we find it promptly applied to the group, any group. We had that already in the beginning with the antique Maximum Doctrine of the Physiocrats, and then with modern welfare economics. Now we should have it still, but with a better modern, and at the same time properly traditional, conscience, giving complete courage for what follows. That contains mathematics which is unusual and original in itself, so as to give interest regardless of what otherwise it should be about. An accidental effect is to enhance the credibility of ideas offered at the start.

The voting paradox has prominence, but it is a paradox only if one sees the elected candidate – surely "derived from individual desires", or votes at least – as not simply elected but also best, a social maximum. Since the paradox is not made into a lesson for not seeing elected candidates that way, it becomes the opposite and reinforces the simplistic optimization way of thinking which is important for welfare economics.

A giver of solutions to problems, the mathematical mode is also a problem itself, because of the scientific aura. No strategy is suggested here, but something parallel

---

19 I had the fancy that the same fate was hanging over the economics graduate students at my lecture on "Economic Optimism" given in Stanford, 23 April 1987.

involving the same psychology has been well expressed by Harold Morowitz (1981): "A popular strategy in modern salesmanship is to associate an impressive scientific term with a product. Thus 'protein' has been put into shampoo, 'nucleic acid' into hair rinse – and 'entropy' into economics and sociology".

A group, as understood in choice theory, should be a model that involves individuals and their connections, not just an abstract set. The model should be explicit about its features, so that it is known what is being dealt with: there are the individuals and, moreover, there is what they have to do together. Here the matter is just terminology, but there can be obscurity in arguments dealing with a group about what it is that makes the individuals into a group.

In the familiar economic model, there are individual agents whose connection with each other rests solely on the fact that they trade goods at certain prices. They take notice only of prices and encounter each other only because, so we understand, wherever there is a buyer there must be a seller and conversely. These individuals, though a group by virtue of the transaction connections, have no purpose or other government other than their own separate ones, by which they voluntarily enter into the transactions; the only interface between them is the price. In the model they have no community but prices – no political connection, and no other expression of a common interest. The model even lacks the terms that might provide a definition of group welfare and give it a significant function. But still group welfare is talked about. One should wonder how this is possible. It might be possible to envision a model that included some concept of group welfare, but it would be a different model.

In microeconomics, an economy is a model consisting of a group of individuals who form a system through their transaction relationships. Political theory might take a political body to comprise a group of individuals bound together by a constitution. For purposes of ideal discussion, economic and political aspects may be isolated from each other, even though in experience they are bound together; desiccated idealizations are better for purposes of abstract discussion. We have theory that deals with the characteristics of groups of individuals making group decisions based on individual decisions, as in democratic processes. The theory might relate primarily to politics, but it has come to be applied as well to economics, where, though there can be doubts that it should, it is linked with welfare theory.

Groups of various kinds are found in the world of experience, and they make group decisions – a school of dolphins, flight of geese, sport team, military unit, biological population, society of cells in an organism and so forth. One can compare a political body or economic system with such groups for similarities and contrasts. Some decisions taken by these groups may be comprehensible and others mysterious, but in any case we would not think of interpreting all their decisions as simple optimization.

3 Keynes on "National self-sufficiency"

3.1 FREE TRADE

> But when we wonder what to put in its place, we are extremely perplexed.
>
> Keynes

International relations have been well known for instability, resulting in break-downs that lead to military confrontation. Today counterbalancing these traditional tensions are additional ecological, environmental and population concerns, as well as the intense involvement in trade. There may be hope for greater stability, but no guarantee.

There is the familiar pattern where nationalities, markets and religions bind masses of people together – and contribute to conflicts. States require a basis of security for viability. Hence outside threats are matched by measures of defence, which in turn give a capability for offence, feeding new needs for defence, creating an expanding, exhausting cycle. This is the typical destabilization pattern, and economic relationships can fall victim to it when things go wrong.

The expanding spiral has been at the root of difficulty about disarmament, mak-ing it not quite feasible. But the major powers now have the deterrence of the bomb, and they suffer exhaustion from the demands of the spiral without having reached the point of war. There is something like the appearance of a new situation.

It may seem that almost anything can be thought or said in economics and probably has been. Now there is the suspicion that, as a result of volatilities enhanced by electronics, which allow massive movements of capital almost instan-taneously, perhaps just by chance, an instability of a new order may be creeping into the system – one that may at some point test the robustness of the system, or demonstrate its fragility.

Trade seems to be the order of the day. The current emphasis is on the gains from trade, expansion is an understood condition for prosperity, and free trade (nebu-lously, whatever it should mean, since in practice trade is always hedged in by all sorts of rules and regulations) is held up by the more determined traders as the ideal.

Few try to imagine what a world of truly open markets and free trade would be like – the befuddlement with global noise, the unrelieved stress from adjusting to movements and dealing with clever manoeuvres. Alternatively, there is the view of the market as invisible hand or as a medium for coordinating supply and demand. According to this view, the market is just a machine that does not notice what it does. It is driven by gain and not everything that happens is open and friendly. Hence, understandably, when it is possible, wherever there is a sovereign community and not just a trading post, there is resort to 'protectionism'.

It is possible to be in favour of peace without being sure what should be done with it. George Ignatieff[20] argued that cutting back armaments can serve a country's competitiveness in the world market. If that should be the result of peace, it could be a matter of jumping from the frying pan into the fire. The problem of peace, which once meant how to attain peace in the first place, now may take on an additional meaning. Peace once attained will not be without its own difficulties.

The building of self-sufficiency in some sense, or viability without completely haphazard dependence on others, is an alternative worthy of consideration by those who would know how to enjoy it. It could affect development policy, which so often promotes trade interests under the guise of aid.

Protecting borders is called defence, something understandable and common-place, even good. However, protecting an economic community is 'protection-ism' – not so good! Yet the alternative to economic protectionism is to be exposed to arbitrary happenings that do not serve home interests, that absorb attention and require continual and costly adjustments beyond the capacity of many, who then fall into a disadvantaged position. The promotion of free trade as an ideal and an unqualified good, besides the falsity in it, in effect covers over issues that should require deliberation. Such teachings in any case tend to be disregarded by those with practical responsibilities, so it is to some extent inconsequential. The doctrine of free trade is like those portentous and hazy formulae or slogans that bolstered claims of the recently abandoned communist ideology. Nonetheless, as in that case, it does have significant influence and invites contrary thinking. For that the 1933 article of Keynes does service, even though he had been concerned about peace at a time when its preservation seemed unlikely. He reopens ideas where teachings aided by objectionable argument would have them closed. Unless indicated otherwise all following quotations are from that article.

3.2   EXTERNAL AFFAIRS

I thought England's free-trade convictions, maintained for nearly a hundred years, to be both the explanation before man and the justification before heaven of her economic supremacy.

Keynes

While once one would usually have gone to market for a few things largely of local origin, today we are in the midst of a global system, one without respect for

20 Holtom Lecture, Ottawa, 6 February 1989.

locality. There is nothing wrong with markets as such, where goods are traded or bear a price. They are not the discovery of modern economics but have always existed, coming into being wherever there has been some protection of property. Traders, as such, must find the market a good thing, but no one long ago said it was 'optimal', whatever that may mean. Access to a market opens opportunity. There may then be a temptation, but whether or not to yield to it should still be a question.

According to Keynes, "to shuffle out of the mental habits of the nineteenth century world is likely to be a long business". These habits still persist and one may wonder whether the shuffle can have a quicker pace. They were the habits of the undisputed economic rulers of that era, Britain and then the United States, that gave confident approval to the "survival of the economically fittest", themselves.[21] In view of changes in the world, some other thoughts should probably be admitted.

> I sympathize ... with those who would minimize, rather than with those who would maximize, economic entanglement between nations.
>
> Keynes

This idea is at odds with normal thinking, and certainly with surrender to indiscriminate globalization. But the guard at a frontier does not only have to watch for an invasion of troops; anything that would cross can be inspected. When the division of labour is freely extended internationally, the frontier is opened and an element of sovereignty and security has been given up.

Communities are formed by people living and acting together, with common interests for pursuit and protection. They share in the care and defence of a territory, and enjoy the resulting security, create a market for the division of labour, or are united in other ways. However that may be, a community, perhaps just a village, even a club, is marked by separateness from the outside.

In the dependence of welfare of a country on external relationships, defence is a branch, and there one thinks first of the military. This takes away from other aspects, such as economic. However, in the age of deterrence through mutually assured destruction, military exercise is restricted, if not prevented, and relationships between countries are confined more to economics. Functions of defence are transferred to the economic sphere, and inert military weight could become a debility.[22]

In his 1933 article Keynes is concerned about defence where the military is not given high priority, and about peace. This is not 'Keynesian economics'; rather it seems to be an isolated offering that he did not pursue further. Most of what has happened more recently is in the opposite direction, but that does not alter the value of it.

---

21 The Japanese are of course successful traders, even a model nowadays, though they seem not to be at all doctrinaire about it.

22 Written over a decade ago before 9/11.

The self-sufficiency envisaged cannot, of course, be understood in any completely simple sense, but it includes the idea that it is better not to have a way of life where one is at the mercy of others for important essentials; for these, Keynes give importance to proximity. Priorities may produce stages of community, anything outside at any stage being more expendable than anything within. Since the Earth itself is not expendable, there has to be some pulling together at that, the final stage.

3.3   PROXIMITIES

Let goods be homespun.

Keynes

The Earth is a community now that any part of it can be reached from any other in a few hours, and it is especially that since its destruction would affect everyone. People become associated by proximity; friends, and enemies, are usually neighbours. There are many kinds of distances, but geographical location reduces them, making it, as it has always been, especially important. Territories have been delineated by oceans, rivers and mountains, besides other accidents of history.

A definition of self-sufficiency cannot be simple at this particular time, though new factors might now serve the idea better. Images of the old city-state, or the Virgilian agricultural estate, may not fit entirely though they have something to offer. But in any case it would be helpful now to understand Keynes's concept of national self-sufficiency, and why he advocated it. In particular, Keynes proposed proximity of producers and consumers, and of the owners and operators of productive facilities. This is at variance with wisdom of 1933 and today.

Proximity may be understood to serve sovereignty, which usually, in the first place, has a territory as reference, and the security of some degree of sufficiency. Regional deficiencies can be diminished by trading in a community; but a community as a whole may itself have deficiencies. Hence communities have reasons for getting together, as it were in a hierarchy providing progressive extensions of home. Collective concern for the Earth, the final home extension, imposes a community over all others; whatever the deficiencies there, they have to be lived with, since there is (as yet) nowhere else to go.

Keynes remarked on various political experiments going on around the world. He preferred self-determination over mutual interference, whereby communities might sink or swim as they choose. The needs of community may produce some convergence of elements, but the divergence into variety is in the order of things and has claim: as might be allowed, every specific locus is unique and has its peculiar entitlement and sovereignty.

3.4 DISTANCES

Remoteness between ownership and operation is an evil.

Keynes

Dependence on others in some vital matter, especially when it is not reciprocal, leaves one disadvantaged and exposed. The destruction of the Adelaide market (see last section), which can be interpreted in other ways, is a good example. The oil embargo demonstrates the case of import-dependence and its hazard. Similarly there is export-dependence, at an unfortunate extreme in the case of single-crop economies. Economic vulnerability can lead to unsettlement and wreckage comparable to that from military assault. Yet economic defence is not taken as seriously as military defence, and not given the same approval.

Keynes questions the "great concentration of national effort on the capture of foreign trade ... the penetration of a country's economic structure by the resources and the influence of foreign capitalists" and the "close dependence of our own economic life on the fluctuating economic policies of foreign countries". He finds nothing here to serve stability and peace. In a scheme of things "which aims at the maximum international specialization and at the maximum geographical diffusion of capital wherever the seat of ownership", the "protection of a country's foreign interests, the capture of new markets" and "the progress of economic imperialism" are unavoidable. Coherent proximities are spoilt, and life is exposed to remote disturbances and dreadful complications. He goes further, objecting to other incoherencies and distances:

> The divorce between ownership and the real responsibility of management is serious ... when, as a result of joint-stock enterprise, ownership is broken up between innumerable individuals who buy their interest today and sell it tomorrow and lack altogether both knowledge and responsibility towards what they momentarily own ... I am irresponsible towards what I own and those who operate what I own are irresponsible towards me.

He illustrates this idea with "the part ownership of A.E.G. of Germany by a speculator in Chicago, or of municipal improvements of Rio de Janeiro by an English spinster". In allowing that "There may be some financial calculation which shows it to be advantageous that my savings should be invested in whatever quarter of the habitable globe shows the greatest marginal efficiency of capital or the highest rate of interest", he brings forward neglected factors "which will bring to nought the financial calculation". He cedes possible merit, in its time, to the general presumptions regarding the fundamental characteristics of economic society that prevailed since the nineteenth century, and declares, "I become doubtful whether the economic cost of national self-sufficiency is great enough to outweigh the other advantages of gradually bringing the producer and the consumer within the ambit of the same national, economic and financial organization".

Then he further states:

> Experience accumulates to prove that most modern mass-production processes
> can be performed in most countries and climates with almost equal efficiency.
> Moreover, as wealth increases, both primary and manufactured products play
> a smaller relative part in the economy compared with houses, personal services
> and local amenities which are not subject to the international exchange; with
> the result that a moderate increase in the real cost of the former consequent on
> greater national self-sufficiency may cease to be of serious consequence when
> weighed in the balance against advantages of a different kind. National self-
> sufficiency, in short, though it costs something, may be becoming a luxury
> which we can afford if we happen to want it.

If that was at all true in his time, it could be more so now, and in the future.

Ecology brings forward the notion of the relationship between people and their
territory, fostered by decentralization towards small units. People are not so much
owners as caretakers. Resources are limited, so human needs must be limited too;
insatiability comes from an increasing population and competitive pressures. In
the absence of such raw factors that undermine it, and given the needed character
for the undertaking, any people can, in their own way, build from subsistence
towards satiation – a state that meets their own needs while not undermining those
of the Earth.

3.5   HIGH POINTS

> The intelligence which proceeds not by hoping for the best (a method only
> valuable in desperate situations), but by estimating what the facts are, and
> thus obtaining a clearer vision of what to expect.
>
> Pericles

Not only capitalism, with its global market free of any regulation but its own, but
also Marxism has its high point in the "withering away of the state", under strange
assumptions about the nature of man, discussed by J. Alvey.[23] The two share a
similarity on this point, even though the one withering may not be quite the other.
As for any principle that may be drawn from Keynes's own article, if there is
one, it is proximity, it is having the sense needed for coming down to Earth – an
important proximity. He gives this principle several applications. It may not join
with the sublimities of Leibniz and Hegel, but in sober times it may be enough.

23 The relevance of Marx's assumptions on the nature of man for his economics. *Research Paper* No.
    314 (April 1987), School of Economic and Financial Studies, Macquarie University, North Ryde,
    NSW.

Keynes seems to have in mind an order different from what we have, even though he does not provide details.

What is the purpose of Keynes's order and how should it come about? He submits it is not an end in itself but is "directed to the creation of an environment in which other ideals can be safely and conveniently pursued". He sees the emergence as gradual: "It should not be a matter of tearing up roots but of slowly training a plant to grow in a different direction". Considering the field for the training, this may be an optimistic way of putting it. With regard to a future order, time with its normal dispensation of disaster may bring it about in the shape of repairable fabrics that survive. But Keynes seems to think that, after "estimating what the facts are", there is a path that should be taken anyway.

Clearly his views could have no impact at the time. He seems to have disregarded for the momentum of the present, choosing instead to give his view of what economics must eventually be about. His ideas relate not just to the concerns he had in 1933, but to the present day and the future. "Estimating what the facts are", for Keynes, most immediately concerned the oncoming world war, while now the world-encircling realities have to do with interdependent factors of ecology, environment and population.[24]

3.6 INTERESTS

Current issues were highlighted in a debate on the public television programme "American Interest", one side taken by the chairman of Citizens against Foreign Control of America (C.A.F.C.A.), June-Collier Mason. The opponent advanced the usual unreconstructed dogmas about gains from trade, while Mason held that not everything was for sale, or could be bought. It seemed a questionable evolution when states vie with each other for foreign investments or purchases, even though one knows the usual arguments: to create jobs, stimulate the economy, transfer technology and so on. There could be a need met and a gain obtained, but one can wonder where this will lead if the drive continues – as with drug dependence. There must be things that an independent people should do for themselves, and the spectacle makes any concept of self-sufficiency seem empty. But we may just be witnessing the *reductio ad absurdum* of the unqualified free trade indoctrination, preachers themselves now being principal victims.

Next to this phenomenon, for contrast, one can contemplate how Japan, now the trader, once withdrew from the international scene for about 260 years. It took gunboats to make them open up – for trade, of course.

The old forms of national power, backed by the military, have not been attenuated but transmuted and channelled elsewhere, preserving the usual potential for coercion and conflict. Economics is as serious as war and closely related to it. The Peloponnesian War was precipitated by the denial of the Athens market to an ally

---

24 Apparently more now following 9/11.

of Sparta, and it took an American gunboat to persuade the Japanese into trade relations. Apparently Keynes was not satisfied with the concept of what constitutes peace and was looking further.

His exploration may be understood better today than in 1933, for many reasons. It is not related to "Keynesian economics" which Axel Leijonhufvud[25] has distinguished from "the economics of Keynes", or to anything that one usually associates with Keynes; rather it has to do with a neglected item.

---

25 *Keynesian Economics and the Economics of Keynes.* New York: Oxford University Press, 1968.

4 In Adelaide (or anywhere)

> Not only do I have an apparently eccentric fondness for an ancient economic
> institution, but I am led to strange political conclusions.
>
> Michael Symons (1987)

An important kind of market is the local one, associated with and requiring the
protection of a specific community. Giants stride the global market seeking entry
where they choose, destroying local fabric wherever they go. Their unhampered
access can only be explained by the unguardedness of victims.

Michael Symons (1987) describes an illustrative case where the East End market
in Adelaide, South Australia, was being demolished and moved to the outskirts.
The change would serve the interests of large-scale producers, merchants, super-
markets, food processors and the developers of the valuable city site. At the same
time, "food [would] lose cheapness, freshness, quality and seasonality". After
some pressure, the Edwardian facades were retained, as a "heritage case". However, "a market is more than a building, being a key gastronomic, agricultural,
economic and civic institution". Adelaide is to be locked another step into the
national and international distribution system:

> Just as the shift will hasten the demise of small market gardeners and
> orchardists, so too will more greengrocers be forced out of business by the
> greater distances, changed hours and much higher rents. Supermarkets, which
> presently by-pass the East End market, can be accommodated at the new
> 32-hectare centre.
>
> So, we will lose a few more primary producers, market workers and corner
> greengrocers: Adelaide citizens will get more expensive, older and lower-
> quality fruit and vegetables (try shopping at our supermarkets now) and, more
> profoundly, we will further lose seasonal and regional variation in our food.

The costs and benefits and their incidence are well outlined in this description.
The global market acts as a destructive solvent, corroding and carrying away local
particulars. Its work could have been stopped, but the accepted teaching has given

it an inevitability and legitimacy, numbing thought and persuading submission. How else can one explain "why farmers, who so often complain they are ignored, aren't protesting at the loss of their city presence, and their livelihoods? Why aren't small retailers rioting against unfair competition, and unemployment? Why don't governments care about eaters"?

The destruction of *Les Halles* markets in Paris is compared with razing Notre Dame Cathedral, leaving Parisians with more expensive, inferior produce: "A vital cuisine is derived from the basic level of the myriad activities of individual operators – not from food giants. So when the East End market goes the way of *Les Halles* and Covent Garden, Adelaide will lose a colourful centre and, more importantly, the original free market".

As said by Fernand Braudel, "markets are the *raison d'être* of towns. They are the birthplace of our economy". A society fails when it allows its markets to be destroyed because of excessive love of polemicist theoreticians. As, rather like the monotheistic dedication, these envisage a single being, the Market (these days global though hitherto not so specific), as ground for all economy and endow it with the divine Optimum – it was supposed the age of faith had passed but apparently not!

Zealous devotees of the market system, missing the simple point of it and pursuing a new theory dressed with equations and permeated with "unjustified scientism"[26] and worse, may be its enemies. Thinking of a market which is "perfect" or "optimal" or whatever, they advocate a chaotic abandonment of restraint and offer less in the way of discipline that could serve the system and its genuine welfare aspects.

Bibliography

Adelman, Ken (1989). Alan Gotlieb: on being a diplomat (interview). *Ottawa MAGAZINE*, March.

Afriat, S. N. (1965). People and population. *World Politics* 17, 3, 431–9. Japanese translation, with foreword by Edwin O. Reischauer: *Japan–America Forum* 11, 10 (October), 1–28.

—— (1972). Reservations about market sovereignty: four notes. In R. A. Mundell (Ed.) *Policy Formation in an Open Economy*. Proceedings of the conference at the University of Waterloo, Ontario: Waterloo Research Institute.

—— (1980). *Demand Functions and the Slutsky Matrix*. Princeton Studies in Mathematical Economics, 7. Princeton: Princeton University Press.

—— (1987a). Economic Optimism. Lecture, Economics Department, Stanford University, 21 April; and in Australia, May–June: ANU, Macquarie, Melbourne, Sydney, Newcastle.

---

26 Valuable phrase found in a Report of the Institute in Princeton.

—— (1987b). *Logic of Choice and Economic Theory*. Oxford: Clarendon Press.

—— (1988). Optimism from Leibniz to Modern Economics. Sophia University, Tokyo, 27 April.

—— (1989). On Trade and Self-sufficiency. Institute of Economics and Management Science, Kobe University, 22 April 1988. Revised version: *Research Paper* No. 326 (April 1989), School of Economic and Financial Studies, Macquarie University, New South Wales.

—— (1994). Market & Myth. 2nd International Conference, The Society for Social Choice and Welfare, University of Rochester, New York, July 8–11.

—— (1999). In the Economic Context: Concerning Efficiency. Symposium 'On Effectiveness', Centre for Interdisciplinary Research on Social Stress, San Marino (Republic of San Marino), 20–25 May 1999. *Quaderno* No. 254 (May), Department of Political Economy, University of Siena.

—— (1999). Market Equilibrium and Stability. *Quaderno* No. 264 (September), Department of Political Economy, University of Siena.

Allaby, Michael and Peter Bunyard (1980). *The Politics of Self-Sufficiency*. Oxford University Press.

Allison, Graham (1989). Success is Within Reach. *New York Times*, 19 February.

Alvey, J. (1984). John Maynard Keynes and his relevance for today. *Economic Analysis and Policy* 14, 1 (March), 98–118.

—— (1986). Keynes: fifty years later. *Australian Society*, December 4–5.

—— (1987a). John Locke's Theory of Property. *Working Paper in Economics* No. 62 (March), Department of Economics, University of Queensland.

—— (1987b). The Relevance of Marx's Assumptions on the Nature of Man for his Economics. *Research Paper* No. 314 (April) School of Economic and Financial Studies, Macquarie University, Sydney, North Ryde, NSW.

Arrow, K. J. (1951). *Social Choice and Individual Values*. New York: John Wiley. 2nd edition 1963.

Bell, Daniel and Irving Kristol (1982). *The Crisis in Economic Theory*. New York: Basic Books.

Beckerman, Wilfred (1974). *In Defence of Economic Growth*. London: Jonathan Cape.

Boulding, Kenneth E. (1963). The Legitimation of the Market (mimeo). Lecture delivered at Rice University, Houston, Texas.

Braudel, Fernand (1981). *Civilisation and Capitalism*. New York: Harper and Rowe.

Brecher, Irving and Donald J. Savoie (Eds) (1993). *Equity and Efficiency in Economic Development: Symposium in honour of Benjamin Higgins*. Montreal: McGill-Queen's University Press.

Cassidy, John (1996). The Decline of Economics. *The New Yorker*, 2 December, 50–60.

De Villiers, Henri (1989). Quoted in *TIME*, March 27, p. 42.

Deane, Phyllis (1978). *The Evolution of Economic Ideas*. Cambridge: Cambridge University Press.

Galbraith, J. K. (1973). *Economics and the Public Purpose*. Boston: Houghton Mifflin.

Gao, Jinbao (1987). The reform of the Chinese economic system (mimeo). Lecture delivered at Dunmore Lang College, Macquarie University, NSW, May.

George, Susan (1988). *A Fate Worse Than Debt*. Harmondsworth: Penguin.

Goldsmith, Edward (1980). Thermodynamics or Ecodynamics. *Ecologist*, 178–95.

—— (1984). *The Social and Economic Effects of Large Dams*. San Francisco: Sierra Club Books.

Hansen, Bent and Girgis A. Marzouk (1965). *Development and Economic Policy in the UAR (Egypt).* Amsterdam: North-Holland.

Hayek, F. A. (1974). The Pretence of Knowledge. Nobel Memorial Lecture, Stockholm, 11 December. In Hayek (1978). Chapter 2.

Hayek, F. A. (1976). The Atavism of Social Justice. The 9th R. C. Mills Memorial Lecture, University of Sydney, 6 October. In Hayek (1978). Chapter 5.

—— (1978). *New Studies in Philosophy, Politics, Economics and the History of Ideas.* Chicago: University of Chicago Press.

Heilbroner, Robert (1972). *The Worldly Philosophers.* New York: Simon and Schuster.

Higgins, Benjamin (1993). Equity and efficiency in development: basic concepts. In Brecher and Savoie (1993). Chapter 1.

Holdren, John P. (1990). Energy in transition. *Scientific American* 263, 3 (September), 156–63.

Hutchison, T. W. (1977). *Knowledge and Ignorance in Economics.* Chicago: University of Chicago Press.

Ipsen, Eric (1997). Capitalism's King Spies Evil in Market-Mad Realm. *International Herald Tribune*, January 16, pp. 1 and 6.

Keynes, J. M. (1933). National Self-Sufficiency. *The New Statesman and Nation*, 8 and 15 July; *The Yale Review*, Summer; *Collected Writings*, Vol. XXI, 233–46.

—— (1982). *The Collected Writings of John Maynard Keynes.* D. Moggridge (Ed.). London: Macmillan.

Kuttner, Robert (1985). The Poverty of Economics: a report on a discipline riven with epistemological doubt on the one hand and rigid formalism on the other. *Atlantic Monthly*, February.

Leijonhufvud, Axel (1968). *Keynesian Economics and the Economics of Keynes.* New York: Oxford University Press.

—— (1973). Life among the Econ. *Western Economic Journal* 11, 3 (September); reprinted in Dimand (1986).

Marzouk, Girgis A. (1972). *Economic Development and Policies: Case Study of Thailand.* Foreword by Jan Tinbergen. Rotterdam University Press.

Mason, J.-C. (1987a). The trade war is on; we must fight to win. *USA Today*, 1 April.

—— (1988b). Foreign money is bad for USA. *USA Today*, August 17.

McMurtry, John (1988). The unspeakable: understanding the system of fallacy in the media. *Informal Logic* X.3 (Fall), 133–50.

—— (1990). Education for Sale. *CAUT Bulletin* 37, 7 (September), pp. 11 and 15.

Mishan, E. J. (1981). *Economic Efficiency and Social Welfare.* London: Allen & Unwin.

—— (1986). *Economic Myths and the Mythology of Economics.* Brighton, Sussex: Wheatsheaf Books.

Morowitz, Harold (1981). Review of Entropy, a New World View by Jeremy Rivkin and Ted Howland. In *Discover*, January, 83–5.

Samuelson, Paul A. (1970). Maximum Principles in Analytical Economics. Nobel Memorial Lecture, Stockholm, 11 December. In *Les Prix Nobel en 1970.* Amsterdam and New York: Elsevier; reprinted in *Science*, 10 September 1971.

Schumpeter, Joseph A. (1954). *History of Economic Analysis.* New York: Oxford University Press.

Scientific American (1990). Special Issue: Energy for Planet Earth. Volume 263, 3 (September).

Settle, Thomas (1976). *In Search of a Third Way.* Toronto: McLelland & Stewart.

Shubik, Martin (1970). A Curmudgeon's guide to microeconomics. *Journal of Economic Literature* 18, 2.

Soros, George (1997). The capitalist threat. *Atlantic Monthly*, February, 45–58.

Symons, Michael (1987). In Adelaide, the Collapse of the Free Market. Sydney, NSW: *Times on Sunday*, 3 May, p. 35.

Tarascio, Vincent J. (1986). The crisis in economic theory: a sociological perspective. *Research in the History of Economic Thought and Methodology* 4, 283–95.

Tobin, J. (1987). On the efficiency of the financial system. *Lloyds Bank Review* 183 (July), 1–15.

Ukai, Yasuharu (1987). Cycles of isolationism and foreign trade – a case study of Japan. *Kansai University Review of Economics and Business* 16, 1 (September), 61–74.

Part VI

In the economic context: concerning 'efficiency'

Prepared for the symposium 'On Effectiveness' organized by the Centre for Inter-disciplinary Research on Social Stress, San Marino (Republic of San Marino), 20–25 May 1999, reproduced now with permission of C.I.R.O.S.S.

The study of terminology related to 'effectiveness' may range in different areas where there are differences in ideas and usage. Comparisons being wanted, here the concern is with topics more or less related to economics. It is suitable to deal with 'efficiency' which in that context is the term with proximity to 'effectiveness' and often replaces it. After attention to the general use of terms, a review is made of branches. These may have to do with such topics as production, consumption, cost and benefit, games, choice theory, welfare economics, and the market.

In dealing with any 'effectiveness', one should like to know what it is that has it, and also what it is for. It must be possessed by a specific thing, in relation to a specific outcome. At least, that is a position that has entertainment here.

The possibilities may be either complete effectiveness or complete ineffectiveness, a hit or miss, as in some cases. Otherwise the effectiveness could be to some intermediate extent. A medical treatment works to bring about cure of an illness, with success or failure as outcome, in some instances, and in others an intermediate result may be recognized. A further complication may have to do with side-effects, or joint-products, and these could be important. For instance, there could be prejudice in favour of keeping the patient alive.

Hence with 'effectiveness' there is always an agency in view, and an objective. This is a pattern for the term to be recognized. It should be mentioned since, as will be noticed, without having some such pattern in full view there can be an easy drift into obscurity.

Besides 'effectiveness' our undertaking has also to do with 'efficiency'. Everything said so far about 'effectiveness' could be said here also. In a way, therefore, these terms are synonyms, or at least closely related. If a difference between them should be found, it might be in respect to context factors which influence use. Which term is used may convey a message about context. Complexities with the terms which come into view in Symposium papers dealing with other areas are not present in economics.

At this point to gain settlement concerning proximity, if that should be needed, let us consult '*Pitman's Book of Synonyms and Antonyms*' (4th edn, 1949). Under 'Efficient' it says: See 'Effective'. And under 'Effective' is a list that includes 'Efficient'.

The terms may be virtual synonyms but can still have a difference. The magazine "Health and Efficiency" could not just as well have been called Health and Effectiveness, at least, not with the same tone or expectation about contents. In reference to some mechanical engine one would expect efficiency to have some straightforward definition, like miles/gal, or, if it be a steam-engine, conversion of heat into mechanical energy. But for effectiveness of the engine, one might have to regard it as a tool and ask what it is supposed to do. At least, not break down too often. Perhaps more likely, one might deal with effectiveness of an economic policy, or of a social programme. In any case, words can have a looseness, and the user some liberty.

But still, respect for common usage has importance. This has an appearance in the case where 'rationality' is taken to be nothing else than a maximization, or optimization; in other words, a sort of efficiency. However, referring again to Pitman's Synonyms and Antonyms, under 'Rational' it shows "Sane, intelligent, reasonable, intellectual". That does not settle the matter, as would be gathered from history of a seminar on 'Rationality' that has been going on in Paris for years. There could be hazard of something like the same fate for 'Efficiency'. Another case, to have more attention, is where "Pareto Optimum", in a retreat from a dubious usage, becomes replaced by "Pareto efficient", as if this made any difference.

Issues to do with efficiency and effectiveness may be recognized and well understood by many. However, like the power of reason, such appreciation should not be completely taken for granted. A new manager, brought in to modernize a certain hotel in a certain country, encountered unexpected obstacles to reforms he proposed for the sake of what he viewed as improved efficiency. No one understood what he was driving at. The only reason anyone understood for the way of doing anything was that it had always been done that way. It was similar with the preacher who insisted that piety did not lie in doing anything because it was reasonable.

The study "Effectiveness and Efficiency: a comparison between settled agriculturists and semi-nomadic agro-pastoralists in Eastern Sudan" by Giorgio Ausenda deals with two social groups, in two aspects, first, "the 'effectiveness' of each group in achieving a life secure from natural unforeseens by the production and storage of a greater quantity of food", and second, "the 'efficiency' of each social group in maintaining the continuity of the group itself". In either case, as required, there is a statement of the objective in view. The objectives are different but with fair acceptance the same single term might have been used. However, use of both terms enables an understanding about which objective is being talked about.[1]

The two attributes for the two groups have magnitudes, based on data, and it is to be seen "whether and in what way they are related". Here is recognition of a scale of achievement for either of the objectives.

In some contexts the measurement may have undecided or arbitrary aspects, or present some kind of a problem. For instance, ranking treatments for an illness can become complicated by allowance for side-effects. Or an industrial process, once declared efficient, loses favour after an environmental impact study.

Any dealing with efficiency can raise the question of how it should be measured. There has to be an objective in view, and so a preference order on outcomes – which may or may not be represented numerically – deciding the extent to which the objective is achieved.

To be efficient without further qualification is to achieve the objective to the greatest extent possible, and to arrive at the *optimum*, and to proximity with the

---

1   I have to respect the disagreement of Giorgio Ausenda about this view.

language of *choice* and *preference* and of *utility* and *welfare* found in economics. Our undertaking is to report on features in this area where efficiency is certainly important, if not a most central idea. This brings forward "welfare economics", the welfare and efficiency theory or doctrine about the market, highly peculiar to economics and a main focus of what we have to consider.

An interesting phase in the review of terminology is the consideration of its abuses. The 'optimism' associated with economics, and with Leibniz, gives the term a claim for attention, but more straightforward matters will be dealt with first. Concern with some form of effectiveness or efficiency is widespread, in every kind of connection, and gives rise to questions about procedure, concept, method, standards, definitions and so forth. This is brought out by deliveries at the Symposium, beside being no doubt a cause for having it in the first place.

A *cost–benefit analysis* deals with some project, a road, bridge, hospital or whatever, which provides a benefit and has a cost. There are two questions: first, is it possible to obtain greater benefit with no greater cost? If no, the project is *cost-effective*, providing maximum benefit obtainable with the given cost constraint. Second, is it possible to obtain as much benefit at a lower cost? If no, the project is *cost-efficient*, obtaining the given benefit at minimum cost.

The terms efficient and effective have a difference here, which might appear to deny they are synonyms. However, they are employed to distinguish two types of efficiency, or effectiveness, just as in the study of the two social groups to which a reference has been made.

Effectivity functions in game theory, introduced by Moulin and Peleg (1982), show another area where 'effectiveness' has made an entry. Such a function describes, for each coalition S, the set of subsets within which S can force an outcome by means of some coordinated action of its members.[2] This use seems in line with expressions about a medical treatment, or some agency or institution, or person, being effective or ineffective, as concerns production of intended outcomes.

Typical economic efficiency concepts have to do with production. In a first notion of a production function f, it determines the output $q = f(x)$ obtained with any inputs $x \in C$.[3] Quite usually now, it instead determines the maximum possible output for the given inputs, so $q \leq f(x)$ for any feasible input–output operation $(x, q) \in C \times \Omega$. The *efficiency* of the operation is then $e = q/f(x)$, that is, actual output as a fraction of the maximum possible. This quotient has also been called the *coefficient of resource utilization*. Necessarily $0 \leq e \leq 1$, with $e = 1$ in the not-so-likely case of a completely efficient operation.

---

2 For awareness of this subject and information about it, I am indebted to Stefano Vannucci, University of Siena, for personal communications in addition to his papers (1999).

3 In present notation, with Ω as the non-negative numbers, $B = \Omega_n$ is the *budget space* (non-negative row vectors), and $C = \Omega^n$ the *commodity space* (column vectors). Then any $P \in B$, $x \in C$ determine $px \in \Omega$ for the cost of the commodity bundle x at the prices p. Sometimes when dealing with a demand function, Ω should be the positive numbers. A scalar always multiplies a row vector on the left and a column vector on the right.

With given production data

$$(x_r, q_r) \in C \times \Omega \quad (r = 1, \ldots, m)$$

econometricians have attempted to estimate a production function f from a non-linear regression of q upon x, to give a close fit for the relation $q_r = f(x_r)$. In this case the errors in the relation come out two sided, positive and negative. However, $q_r \leq f(x_r)$ or one-sided errors would be required of any production function f that represented as feasible the production operations that are actually observed, and given as data. One such function is

$$\hat{f}(x) = \max \left\{ \sum_r q_r t_t : \sum_r x_r t_r \leq x, \sum_r t_r = 1, t_r \geq 0 \right\}.$$

It is on the classical model, monotonic and concave, and if f is any other then $\hat{f}(x) \leq f(x)$ for all x. Hence $\hat{f}$ is the smallest classical function that represents as feasible all the given production operations. This is the *frontier production function*.[4] It determines efficiencies

$$\hat{e}_r = q_r / \hat{f}(x_r).$$

The function is insensitive to data points for which $\hat{e}_r < 1$ and these can be dropped without altering the function. While it has a certain usefulness,[5] this exposes its limitation, to be dealt with again. First there can be comment on the modified function

$$\tilde{f}(x) = \max \left\{ \sum_r q_r t_r : \sum_r x_r t_r \leq x, t_r \geq 0 \right\},$$

which is again classical, being monotonic and concave, and in addition has the conical or constant returns property

$$\tilde{f}(x\sigma) = \tilde{f}(x)\sigma \quad (\sigma > 0).$$

This enables a function representation of the production efficiencies resulting from Farrell's method,[6] these now being

$$\tilde{e}_r = q_r / \tilde{f}(x_r),$$

and such that

$$\tilde{e}_r \geq \hat{e}_r.$$

4 S. N. Afriat, Efficiency estimation of production functions, *International Economic Review* 13, 3 (October 1972), 568–98.
5 It makes a starting point for 'data envelope analysis'. See Note 4 on history.
6 M. J. Farrell, The measurement of economic efficiency, *Journal of Royal Statistical Society*, CXX (Part 3, 1957), 253–81.

These frontier, or envelope, functions are not anything like estimates of a true production function. This is evident from the efficiency distributions they determine for the observed production operations that serve as data, where all the operations to which they are sensitive come out with efficiency 1. For a true function, representing the maximum possible output for any given inputs, it is more acceptable that no observed operations should come out with efficiency 1. A parallel case is illustrative.

Suppose we have speeds v_r of runners over 100 yards and their efficiencies are represented as given by $e_r = v_r/v^*$ where v^* is the greatest speed anyone could run 100 yards. A problem with this concept is that v^* is unknown; athletic records are continually broken, without a sign of finality. The interest now is in an approach to estimation of v^*, which should be greater than any observed v_r. A similar problem concerns heights to which water level rises during floods, in some city.[7] There is the need, in taking preventative measures, to have an estimate of the greatest height that could occur. The approach could also be applicable to the production function, this being understood to determine the unattained greatest possible output for given inputs.

The original approach was based on a model for the distribution of efficiency on the interval [0,1], with density falling to zero at the endpoints, and a single peak, having two parameters to specify location of the peak and concentration around it, determined simultaneously with v^* – or, in the further production application of the idea, simultaneously with the parameters of a production function on some model, originally the Cobb–Douglas – by the method of maximum likelihood. This method, which was a new approach to production function estimation, obtains a *stochastic frontier production function* f^* and a density ρ for the distribution of production efficiency, such that the likelihood of the efficiencies

$$e_r^* = q_r/f^*(x_r)$$

is at a maximum.

Should prices $p \in B$ for the input factors be given, so input $x \in C$ has associated with it a cost px, further efficiency concepts become available, corresponding to the cardinal concepts of cost–benefit analysis, cost-efficiency and cost-effectiveness. These are now formulated in application to a production operation (p, x, q), where output q is produced from inputs x with prices p. Besides the efficiency requirement $q = f(x)$ there are two others, H' and H'', involving the pair (p, x) and the function f. Thus for H'

$$f(x) = \max\{f(y): py \le px\},$$

which is to say

$$py \le px \Rightarrow f(y) \le f(x),$$

7 I am indebted to Ali Doğramacı, Bilkent University, Ankara, for drawing my attention to this similar case.

which corresponds to the *cost-effectiveness* familiar in cost–benefit analysis, and asserts x produces as much as any other input bundle that costs no more at the prices. And for H'',

$$px = \min\{py: f(y) \geq f(x)\},$$

or equivalently,

$$f(y) \geq f(x) \implies py \geq px,$$

which corresponds to *cost-efficiency*, that any input bundle that produces as much as x costs at least as much.

While H' represents *output-maximization*, making x a bundle that has maximum output for the expenditure on input, H'' represents cost-minimization, making x have minimum cost for the output obtained. These are equally compelling basic economic principles. They are generally independent. However, properties of the function f can produce relations between them. For instance, if f is continuous, monotonic increasing, as usual for a classical production function, then they are equivalent, defining a single condition H. Otherwise, H can be defined as the conjunction of the two efficiencies H' and H''. In most matters practice falls short of ideal efficiency, or effectiveness. The condition is therefore too stringent for realistic application. It can be relaxed by introduction of a parameter e, with $0 \leq e \leq 1$, the *level of cost-efficiency*, to make the condition $H'(e)$ defined by

$$f(x) \geq \max\{f(y): py \leq epx\},$$

or equivalently,

$$py \leq epx \implies f(y) \leq f(x),$$

or the condition $H''(e)$ defined by

$$epx \leq \min\{py: f(y) \leq f(x)\},$$

equivalently,

$$f(y) \geq f(x) \implies py \geq epx.$$

While H' requires x to be an input bundle that provides exactly the greatest possible output attainable for its cost, for the more tolerant $H'(e)$ it is enough to obtain at least the output attainable with some fraction e of the cost.

Evidently, for

$$H(e) = H'(e) \wedge H''(e),$$

we have

$$H \Leftrightarrow H(1), \qquad e \geq e'. \implies .H(e) \implies H(e'),$$

since we have this for either of the H' and H'' components, so $H(e)$ becomes progressively more stringent as e is increased, and coincides with the original H for $e = 1$.

Introducing the binary relation $R \subset C \times C$ by

$$x R y \equiv f(x) \geq f(y)$$

this is an order relation, reflexive and transitive,

$$x R x, \qquad x R y R z \Rightarrow x R z.$$

It is the order represented by the function f.[8] The partial efficiency conditions involving (p, x) with the function f now have statements where they depend on f just to the extent of this order,

$$H'(e) \equiv y R x \Rightarrow p y \geq e p x,$$
$$H''(e) \equiv p y \leq e p x \Rightarrow x R y.$$

The classical view of consumption is that it has a measurable utility, which consumers maximize, subject to a budget constraint. A utility function $\phi(x) \in \Omega$ ($x \in C$) shows the utility which results from consumption of, or making use of, any commodities, so it is like a production function, where the product is 'use'. But unlike the production function, the product in this case is not immediately observable.

An observation on the consumer has the form of a demand element $(p, x) \in B \times C$ for which $p x > 0$, showing quantities x obtained at prices p. The cost therefore is $p x$, and in choosing x the consumer should have the maximum utility attainable with this cost. In other words, the demand (p, x), when taken with the utility function ϕ, should be cost-effective,

$$p y \leq p x \Rightarrow \phi(y) \leq \phi(x).$$

A more stringent condition makes x the unique utility maximum subject to the cost constraint, that is,

$$p y \leq p x \wedge y \neq x \Rightarrow \phi(y) < \phi(x).$$

While utility is talked about it is, as said, not in principle directly observable. But it is entertained as the hypothetical determinant of demand behaviour, which is in principle observable. Hence, if utility is to be constructible, it should be on the basis of demand observations. Whether and how it is possible to do that is an old question that has continued to have attention.

Given any collection of demand elements, or *demand correspondence*, $D \subset B \times C$, it can be asked if there exists a utility which represents every element as efficient. If any, there would be many. Originally the utility was understood to be

---

8 With a binary relation R, besides the usual $(x, y) \in R$ because R is a set, also the statements $x R y$, $x \in R y$ or $y \in x R$ are available to assert (x, y) is an element of R, or that x has the relation R to y.

numerically measurable. Then remarks of Pareto about relevance to behaviour lead to emphasis on the "indifference map", or the preference order, free of numerical representation. Any numerical utility ϕ would have effect only to the extent of the *preference order R* represented by it, for which

$$x R y \Leftrightarrow \phi(x) \geq \phi(y),$$

and many functions represent the same order, all those related by a monotonic transformation. Hence, utility should be understood now as given not necessarily by a function but, more significantly, by an order. The utilities that are allowed are those, if any, that can represent given demand observations as showing efficient behaviour.

Consistent with this non-numerical approach Samuelson introduced the "revealed preference" method. According to this, if x was demanded when y was available at no greater cost, then this *reveals* the preference of x over y. In other words, if R is the preference system that governs demand, then, in regard to any demand observation (p, x),

$$(H') py \leq px \Rightarrow x R y,$$

or x is optimal in the cost set. In fact – though he did not put it that way – because he dealt not with a general demand correspondence but with a single-valued demand function, he made x the unique optimum and so had instead the stricter requirement

$$(H^*) py \leq px \wedge y \neq x \Rightarrow x R y \wedge -y R x.$$

From this comes Samuelson's well known "axiom", which was given its needed logical extension by Houthakker. This condition also has the consequence

$$(H'') y R x \Rightarrow py \geq px.$$

For the conjunction

$$H \equiv H' \wedge H'',$$

therefore,

$$H^* \Rightarrow H.$$

The conditions H and H^* determine a relation between a demand element (p, x) and a utility order R, of *compatibility* and *strict compatibility*. While the efficiencies H' and H'' are in general independent, conditions on R produce relations between them, about to be stated.

There is *oversatiation* for R at a point y if a bundle z exists which is less in all amounts but also at least as good, that is,

$$z < y \wedge z R y.$$

The denial of such a possibility, or *insatiability*, requires

$$z < y \Rightarrow -z R y.^9$$

1 If R is complete and xR is closed, then $H'' \Rightarrow H'$.
2 If R is insatiable, then $H' \Rightarrow H''$.
3 If R is representable by a continuous semi-increasing function, then

$H' \Leftrightarrow H''$.

It can be noted that 3 is a consequence of 1 and 2. With the representation by a continuous function, we have the completeness and closure which provides $H'' \Rightarrow H'$ by 1. If also the function is semi-increasing, the insatiability condition in 2 is obtained so that $H' \Rightarrow H''$.

Consequently, for the conjunction H required by compatibility, under such usual conditions we have both $H \Leftrightarrow H'$ and $H \Leftrightarrow H''$. Or in place of the traditional H' of demand analysis, for cost effectiveness or utility maximization, the H'' for cost-efficiency or cost minimization can serve just as well.

Important in Samuelson's approach is the idea – the "revealed preference" principle – that in any act of choice, that is, picking an element out of some set, if x is chosen while some other element y in the set is at the same time available, then we have the preference of x over y, or it is *revealed*. Treated as generally available, as it seems to have been in some hands, the unrestricted principle amounts to taking choice and preference to be synonyms, or to make any choice a result of *efficiency* with respect to some hypothetical objective, or preference system.

---

9 For notation,

$$x \leq y \equiv x_i \leq y_i \text{ for all } i, \quad x \underset{\sim}{<} y \equiv x \leq y \wedge x \neq y, \quad x < y \equiv x_i < y_i \text{ for all } i.$$

A function $\phi(x)$ is *non-decreasing*, *semi-increasing* or *increasing* according to the conditions

$$x \leq y \Rightarrow \phi(x) \leq \phi(y), \quad x < y \Rightarrow \phi(x) < \phi(y), \quad x \underset{\sim}{<} y \Rightarrow \phi(x) < \phi(y).$$

The three different conditions are increasingly restrictive for a continuous function. For a differentiable function ϕ with gradient g they require

$$g \geq 0, \quad g \underset{\sim}{>} 0, \quad g > 0.$$

For an example of the intermediate case, the Leontief type function

$$\phi(x) = \max\{t : at \leq x\} \quad (a \in C)$$

is semi-increasing but not increasing. Representation of utility by a semi-increasing function assures insatiability.

An unrestricted appeal to the revealed preference principle, whereby an efficiency is attributed to elections carried out by voting, leads to the well known "Voting Paradox". Attention to this topic in our dealings with efficiency, though it may not belong strictly to economics, is necessary, and prepares the way for further considerations about groups, in particular about the market economy.

Having an election by means of voting is a way a group of individuals, all of whom might have different ideas about what is good but are still committed to act together, go about making a choice, picking one element out of a set of possibilities, or candidates. The winner is not the best for the group, merely the elected one. Had there been some available prior definition of best candidate, there would have been no need to have an election in the first place. But still we have the Voting Paradox, where there is determination to see the winner as best, and surprise at the result.

Consider three electors A, B, C and three candidates x, y, z. The electors give orders to the candidates, expressing their preferences between them which will determine the votes they cast in elections:

A x, y, z
B y, z, x
C z, x, y

For example, A prefers x to y, so in choice between x and y would choose x, and vote accordingly. Three elections are conducted, running the candidates against each other in pairs:

Election candidates	A, B, C votes	Election results
y, z	yyz	y defeats z
z, x	xzz	z defeats x
x, y	xyx	x defeats y
x, y, z	xyz	none

The added last line is for the inconclusive election in which all candidates run and get one vote each. In the others, the winner defeats the loser with a decisive 2 votes to 1 in each case. For instance, x defeats y, 2 to 1. From this it appears that x is definitely superior to y, for the group, the group being understood to have a preference system, represented by an order relation R, reflexive and transitive. That is, x is as good as y, or xRy, and y definitely not as good as x, or $\sim yRx$, that is, xPy, P being the strict or antisymmetric part of R, necessarily irreflexive and transitive.

Thus we have the cyclical pattern where x defeats y, y defeats z and z defeats x, 2 to 1 in each case. The scheme described is the basis for the well known Voting Paradox. What is a paradox and what else must have been going on in thought to see one here?

paradox (Gr. doxa, opinion) A statement, view, etc., contrary to received opinion; an assertion seemingly absurd but really correct; a self-contradictory statement or phenomenon.

Cassell's *Concise English Dictionary*

A list of the three branches may help the enquiry:

A   A statement, view, etc, contrary to received opinion.
B   An assertion seemingly absurd but really correct.
C   A self-contradictory statement or phenomenon.

The study is useful for present purposes, besides that it serves an understanding of existing thought to know why a paradox has been found.

A promising approach to finding a paradox is to work with (A) from the dictionary statement and entertain a notion about received opinion. We do not have to look far for such a notion in prevailing ideas.

I. *Groups have preferences.* Encouragement comes from the welfare function and efficiency doctrines about a market economy.
II. Preferences are revealed in choices, and with election choices where the winner has definitely more votes than the others, they are strict preferences. That is, the Revealed Preference principle, with a bit added.
III. *Strict preferences are antisymmetric and transitive.* Preferences of the same system belong to an order and so must be transitive as a matter of meaning, and strict preferences are antisymmetric by definition.

If one goes along with that, we do have a paradox. The elections between x, y and y, z reveal the strict preference of x over y and of y over z, or $xPyPz$. One should conclude then, from the transitivity of strict preferences, that x is strictly preferred to z, or xPz. However, the election between x and z shows the opposite, zPx, so there is a contradiction.

The scheme considered is imaginable and so it should be taken seriously. But when the received opinion is brought in a contradiction follows. A possibility is at odds with received opinion and so, according to (A), we have a paradox.

There is nothing to be done about the first side, and so there must be something wrong with the second, the received opinion. A resolution of the paradox is that groups might make choices, possibly by means of elections, but that does not mean they have preferences, and if they do not have preferences then no preferences can be taken to be revealed by any means.

What we have is seemingly absurd if one adheres to the received opinion and is really correct if one does not, so the (B) criteria are met after a fashion. With the adherence we found a preference that must be both present and not present, so giving the self-contradictory phenomenon required by (C). From all sides we have a paradox, if one believes that wherever there are choices they reveal preferences, and then adds the strictness of preference when one candidate has more votes than another. Without the strictness we would have group indifference between all the alternatives, which is consistent with the indecisiveness of the election when all three candidates run together. If that is an escape it takes away from the *main point*, which is simply that the group does not have preferences. Then the elected candidate is not the best candidate, since there is no criterion for the better and worse, but simply the elected candidate; it is the absence of such a criterion that would be cause for having an election in the first place.

A value of settling the well-known paradox is that it has sustaining connections with ideas, in particular about efficiency of the market, whose shortcomings are undramatized by paradox.

A most distinguished authority having to do with efficiency is the philosopher Leibniz who, in his *Théodisée* (1710), takes the Creator as a model. This is where he propounds the doctrine that the actual world is the "best of all possible worlds", chosen by the Creator out of all the possible worlds which were present in his thoughts by the criterion of being the world in which the most good could be obtained at the cost of the least evil. This is the doctrine known as "Optimism"; in its time it drew a great deal of attention, and is famous still. Voltaire's *Candide, ou l'Optimisme* (1759), with the well-known character of Dr Pangloss, was "written to refute the system of optimism, which it has done with brilliant success". This and further information is in the Oxford English Dictionary. It was Leibniz who introduced 'optimum' as a technical term, on the model of a maximum, and it first came into a dictionary in 1752.

As concerns efficiency doctrine related to the market economy, a clue about its beginnings is in historic simultaneity and other coincidences involving Leibniz's Optimism. Though ridiculed by Voltaire and now without influence as such, it found a niche in economics where it has been able to survive with better protection. The arguments about the economy are not quite like that. Instead there is a page of calculus promising infinitesimal precision; it matters not about what, the results are quite the same. This is a parallel of the Maximum Doctrine that came into economics with François Quesnay and the physiocrats and flourishes still. It is impressive to find Quesnay's Economic Principle "greatest satisfaction to be attained at the cost of the least labour-pain" perfectly represented in Leibniz's doctrine *vis-à-vis* the Creator's choice criterion.

The neoclassical outlook originated from the time of Newton and the euphoria over his mechanics, and Leibniz with his Optimism. The economy had then to be approached as a machine, not well understood because nobody around had made it or had the plan. Hence the models economists play with, and the cult of the optimum: "The best is enemy of the good" may be recalled at this point.

BIBLIOGRAPHY

Afriat, S. N. (1964). The Construction of Utility Functions from Expenditure Data. Cowles Foundation Discussion Paper No. 144 (October 1964), Yale University. First World Congress of the Econometric Society, Rome, September 1965. *International Economic Review* 8, 1 (1967), 67–77.

Afriat, S. N. (1965). People and population. *World Politics* 17, 3, 431–9. Japanese translation, with foreword by Ambassador Edwin O. Reischauer: *Japan–America Forum* 11, 10 (October), 1–28.

—— (1968). The construction of cost-efficiencies and approximate utility functions from inconsistent expenditure data. Winter Meeting of the Econometric Society, Washington DC, December.

—— (1971). Efficiency estimation of production functions. Boulder Meetings of the Econometric Society, September 1971. *International Economic Review* 13, 3 (October 1972), 568–98.

—— (1972). Reservations about market sovereignty: four notes. In R. A. Mundell (Ed.) *Policy Formation in an Open Economy*. Proceedings of the conference at the University of Waterloo, Ontario: Waterloo Research Institute.

—— (1973). Collective Decision and Optimality. International Seminar on Public Economics, Siena, Italy, 3–6 September, 1973.

—— (1980). *Demand Functions and the Slutsky Matrix*. Princeton Studies in Mathematical Economics, 7. Princeton: Princeton University Press.

—— (1987a). *Economic Optimism*. Lecture, Economics Department, Stanford University, 21 April. In Australia, May–June: ANU, Macquarie, Melbourne, Sydney, Newcastle.

—— (1987b). *Logic of Choice and Economic Theory*. Oxford: Clarendon Press.

—— (1988a). Efficiency in production and consumption. In Ali Doğramacı and Rolf Färe (Eds). *Applications of Modern Production Theory: Efficiency and Productivity*. Boston: Kluwer-Nijhoff.

—— (1988b). Optimism from Leibniz to Modern Economics. Sophia University, Tokyo, 27 April.

—— (1989). On Trade, and Self-sufficiency. Institute of Economics and Management Science, Kobe University, 22 April 1988. Revised version: *Research Paper* No. 326 (April 1989), School of Economic and Financial Studies, Macquarie University, New South Wales.

—— (1994). Market & Myth. 2nd International Conference, The Society for Social Choice and Welfare, University of Rochester, New York, July 8–11.

—— (1995). The Connection Between Demand and Utility. Department of Economics, European University Institute, Florence, January. Revised version: *Quaderno* 275, Department of Political Economy, University of Siena, December 1999.

—— (1996). Revealed Preference Revealed. Society for the Advancement of Economic Theory Conference on Economic Theory and Applications, Antalya, 16–21 June. Department of Economics, Bilkent University, Ankara, *Discussion Paper* No. 98–7.

—— (1998). Utility Construction – revisited. Department of Economics, Bilkent University, Ankara, *Discussion Paper* No. 98–15.

Arrow, K. J. (1951). *Social Choice and Individual Values*. New York: John Wiley. 2nd edition 1963.

Borts, G. H. and E. J. Mishan (1963). Exploring the uneconomic region of the production function. *Review of Economic Studies* XXIX (October), 289–309.

Brecher, Irving and Donald J. Savoie (Eds) (1993). *Equity and Efficiency in Economic Development: Symposium in Honour of Benjamin Higgins*. Montreal: McGill-Queen's University Press.

Cassidy, John (1996). The Decline of Economics. *The New Yorker*, 2 December, pp. 50–60.

Deane, Phyllis (1978). *The Evolution of Economic Ideas*. Cambridge: Cambridge University Press.

Falk, Richard (1995). *Explorations at the Edge of Time*. Basic Books.

Farrell, M. J. (1957). The measurement of economic efficiency. *Journal of Royal Statistical Society* CXX (Part 3), 253–81.

—— and M. Fieldhouse (1962). Estimating efficient production functions under increasing returns to scale. *Journal of Royal Statistical Society* CXXV (Part 2), 252–67.

Geiss, Charles (1971). Computations of critical efficiencies and the extension of Farrell's method in production analysis. Department of Economics, University of North Carolina at Chapel Hill, mimeograph 1971. Presented at Summer Meeting of the Econometric Society, Boulder, Colorado, September.

Hayek, F. A. (1974). The Pretence of Knowledge. Nobel Memorial Lecture, Stockholm, 11 December. In Hayek (1978), Chapter 2.

—— (1978). *New Studies in Philosophy, Politics, Economics and the History of Ideas.* Chicago: University of Chicago Press.

Heilbroner, Robert (1972). *The Worldly Philosophers.* New York: Simon and Schuster.

Higgins, Benjamin (1989). Equity and efficiency in development: basic concepts. In Brecher and Savoie (Eds) (1992), Chapter 1.

Houthakker, H. S. (1950). Revealed preference and the utility function. *Economica* N. S. 17, 159–74.

Hutchison, T. W. (1977). *Knowledge and Ignorance in Economics.* University of Chicago Press.

Keynes, J. M. (1933). National Self-sufficiency. *The New Statesman and Nation*, 8 and 15 July; *The Yale Review*, Summer; Collected Writings (1982), Vol. XXI, 233–46.

—— (1982). *The Collected Writings of John Maynard Keynes.* D. Moggridge (Ed.). London: Macmillan.

Kuttner, Robert (1985). The Poverty of Economics: A Report on a Discipline Riven with Epistemological Doubt on the One Hand and Rigid Formalism on the Other. *The Atlantic Monthly*, February.

Leijonhufvud, Axel (1968). *Keynesian Economics and the Economics of Keynes.* New York: Oxford University Press.

—— (1973). Life among the Econ. *Western Economic Journal* 11, 3 (September).

Mishan, E. J. (1981). *Economic Efficiency and Social Welfare.* London: Allen & Unwin.

—— (1986). *Economic Myths and the Mythology of Economics.* Brighton, Sussex: Wheatsheaf Books.

Moulin, H. and B. Peleg (1982). Cores of effectivity functions and implementation theory. *Journal of Mathematical Economics* 10, 115–45.

Polanyi, Karl, C. M. Arensberg and H. W. Pearson (Eds) (1957). *Trade and Market in the Early Empires: Economics in History and Theory.* London: Collier-Macmillan.

Samuelson, Paul A. (1948). Consumption theory in terms of revealed preference. *Economica* N. S. 15, 243–53.

—— (1970). Maximum Principles in Analytical Economics. Nobel Memorial Lecture, Stockholm, 11 December. In *Les Prix Nobel en 1970.* Amsterdam and New York: Elsevier. Reprinted in *Science*, 10 September 1971.

Sen, Amartya (1970). *Collective Choice and Social Welfare.* San Francisco: Holden Day.

Settle, Tom (1990). Private communication. Philosophy Department, Guelph University.

Shubik, Martin (1970). A Curmudgeon's guide to microeconomics. *J. Econ. Literature* 18, 2.

Schumpeter, Joseph A. (1954). *History of Economic Analysis.* New York: Oxford University Press.

Slutsky, E. E. (1915). Sulla teoria del bilancio del consumatore. *Giornale degli Economisti* 51 (1915), 1–26. Translation by O. Ragusa: On the theory of the budget of the consumer.

In G. J. Stigler and K. E. Boulding (Eds) *Readings in Price Theory*. Chicago: Richard D. Irwin, 1952. 27–56.

Tobin, J. (1987). On the Efficiency of the Financial System. *Lloyds Bank Review* 183 (July), 1–15.

Vanucci, Stefano (1999a). Effectivity Functions and Parliamentary Governance Structures. University of Siena, *Quaderni del Dipartimento di Economia Politica* No. 240 (January).

—— (1999b). On the Galois lattice of an effectivity function. University of Siena, *Quaderni del Dipartimento di Economia Politica* No. 242 (January).

Varian, Hal R. (1982). The non-parametric approach to demand analysis. *Econometrica* 50, 945–74.

—— (1993). *Microeconomic Analysis*, 3rd edn. W. W. Norton, p. 133.

Volterra, V. (1906). L'economia matematica. Review of Manuele di Economia Politica by V. Pareto. *Giornale degli Economisti* 32, 296–301.

CIROSS/San Marino Symposium

S. N. Afriat, "In the Economic Context: Concerning 'Efficiency'". Università di Siena, Dipartimento di Economia Politica, Piazza S. Francesco, 7, 53100 Siena, Italy.

James Aronson, "What's 'effective', and how to measure it, in restoration ecology". Centre d'Ecologie Fonctionelle et Evolutive (CNRS–UPR 9056), F-34293 Montpellier cedex 5, France.

Giorgio Ausenda, "Effectiveness and Efficiency: a comparison between settled agriculturists and semi-nomadic agro-pastoralists in Eastern Sudan". C.I.R.O.S.S., 6 Contrada San Francesco, San Marino Città, Repubblica di San Marino.

Giuseppe Damiani, "Efficiency and effectiveness in biological systems".

Consiglio Nazionale delle Ricerche, Istituto per la Difesa e la Valorizzazione del Germoplasma Animale (IDVGA-CNR), Palazzo Lita, 20090 Segrate (MI), Italia.

Holger Daun, "In What Should Education Be Effective and How Should It Be Measured"? Institute of International Education, Stockholm University, Sweden.

Peter Messeri, "Defining and Measuring Effectiveness for Health and Human Service Programs". Division of Sociomedical Sciences, The Joseph L. Mailman School of Public Health, Columbia University, New York, NY 10032, USA.

Sanjoy K. Mitter, "On System Effectiveness". Laboratory for Information and Decision Systems and Center for Intelligent Control Systems, Massachusetts Institute of Technology, Cambridge, Mass. 02139, USA.

Riccardo Pozzo, "On the History of the Concept of Effectiveness". School of Philosophy, The Catholic University of America, Washington, DC 20064, USA.

Henry Thompson, "The effectiveness of aid". Japan International Cooperation Agency, JICA-UK Office, 45 Old Bond Street, London WX1 4HS, UK.

Craig A. Tovey, "Effectiveness, Efficiency, and Change in Systems". School of Industrial and Systems Engineering and College of Computing, Georgia Institute of Technology, Atlanta, GA 30332-0205, USA.

John van Willigen, "The Cultural Construction of Efficacy". Department of Anthropology, University of Kentucky, USA.

Notes

Note 1

Aristotle's Value Problem and General Equilibrium

Aristotle sought a basis for the value of things, to enter into his consideration of the 'just exchange'. The things have prices but he does not rest with that measurement, though he is not fully explicit about why not. He has sense of another basis which should have force in his considerations. He gives a word for it, $\chi\rho\varepsilon\iota\alpha$. The meaning this has for Aristotle, if there is a definite one that should be gathered, has retained some obscurity. With the influence of his great authority, the quest for a meaning has gone on persistently over the centuries.

It may be admitted that Aristotle's thought itself is not everywhere fully crystallized, but contains notions that are in a tentative formative stage. Lines of thought linked to Aristotle are in subsequent attempts to establish a further understanding. Two branches may be perceived in the Theory of Value, of Marxist philosophy and the theory of General Equilibrium.

Detached from the later discussions, we return again to the language and argument of Aristotle. The concentration is on a short passage and a single argument where the entry of $\chi\rho\varepsilon\iota\alpha$ is fundamental.[1] Afterwards it may be seen how subsequent thought is able to deal with the quandary Aristotle created for posterity.

An illustrative framework will serve for viewing certain of Aristotle's considerations and arguments. It brings out the nature of some of the difficulties he faced, and also shows a manner for their resolution provided by later developments.[2]

The market represents the opportunity available to any individual for the exchange of goods, at rates specified by ratios of the prices. Since goods are exchangeable with $\mu\nu\alpha\hat{\iota}$, or *minae*, through this medium they become exchangeable with each other, the rates between them being determined by the rates they have with *minae*, that is, their prices. Since a price tells the worth in *minae*, if the price of corn is p_x *minae* per unit, and wine is p_y, then x units of corn and y of wine together have value

$$M = p_x x + p_y y,$$

---

1 Dealt with by A. Afriat (1991).
2 This follows my *Logic of Choice and Economic Theory*. Oxford: Clarendon Press, 1987, pp. 93ff.

in *minae*. Then variations Δx of corn and Δy of wine contribute the value

$$\Delta M = p_x \, \Delta x + p_y \, \Delta y. \tag{1}$$

The amounts Δx of corn and Δy of wine are equal for exchange provided their values $p_x \, \Delta x$, $p_y \, \Delta y$, in *minae* are the same, so they can be bought or sold for the same cost or return, in this amount, and hence exchanged on the market for each other. That is, equating their values in *minae*,

$$p_x \, \Delta x = p_y \, \Delta y$$

or equivalently,

$$\Delta x : \Delta y :: \frac{1}{p_x} : \frac{1}{p_y}.$$

From the public nature of the market, these considerations have validity equally for any individual.

Other exchange rates can also be considered, these instead with a reference that is private for any individual. Suppose an individual attaches another value $u(x, y)$ to the possession of quantities x, y of corn and wine. This value is designated as *utility*, for a significance that will come later though for now that has no importance. When the quantities x, y undergo variations Δx, Δy the variation in utility is

$$\Delta u = u_x \, \Delta x + u_y \, \Delta y, \tag{2}$$

where, for contrast with (1), both the coefficients

$$u_x = \frac{\partial u}{\partial x}, \quad u_y = \frac{\partial y}{\partial y},$$

are functions of x, y.

The goods already have the public *mina*-prices p_x, p_y which are given, and serve in (1), the same for any individual and independent of x, y. Now in (2), the goods also have the utility-prices u_x, u_y with which they are endowed privately by each individual, and have the further variability in that they depend on the amounts x, y of corn and wine already in possession.

A trade between small quantities x, y of corn and wine is 'fair' for this individual, or the loss of one will be exactly compensated by the gain of the other, so to leave utility unaffected, provided

$$\Delta x : \Delta y :: \frac{1}{u_x} : \frac{1}{u_y}.$$

This possible situation exposes difficulties of a type faced by Aristotle in his quest for justice joined with objectivity. The market prices have an outstanding claim as a measurement of value, since they are public and the same for everyone. But they cannot be everything to Aristotle, since he wanted to recognize that goods also have a value from use, apart from the market value, and this use value could vary between individuals. Here it is represented as variable even for a particular individual, depending quite naturally on quantities of the goods already in possession.

Aristotle sought an objectivity for fair exchange, whereas in this picture which gives a modern utility dress to an aspect of his thought – and must be admitted for its possibility and hence be fully accountable – any hope of that may seem vitiated by seemingly quite unalterably divergent subjectivities.

The modern theory, however, does not introduce utility in detachment from its role as governor of individuals, by their pursuit of it to a maximum. With the opportunity for exchange on the market, this maximality requires goods already possessed by an individual to be such as to realize Gossen's law of the proportionality of individual utility prices u_x, u_y to market *minae* prices p_x, p_y.[3] Accordingly,

$$u_x : u_y :: p_x : p_y.$$

This coincidence of exchange rates of any individual with the market exchange rates, and hence also the agreement of exchange rates for all individuals, as now seems to be required in principle, were it offered to Aristotle, might have been welcomed as splendid release from an absorbing dilemma. But for proper satisfaction, there remains an issue to consider.

What has been envisaged is a state of affairs where all buying and selling has been done and no individual would choose to trade further, at the market prices that prevail. It is a question whether the entertainment of such a state is reasonable. There should be some notion of how the economy could enter that state. The theory of general economic equilibrium, originated by Walras[4] and now quite central to economics, provides exactly such a notion.

Suppose, with some disarray in the system, all wanted buying and selling has not been done, at prices that might be entertained. The presence of a market signifies a comprehensive offer for trade at certain prices. But for the offer to be upheld, intentions for trade at those prices have to be satisfiable. In that case, every buyer must find a seller, and every seller a buyer: *aggregate supply must equal aggregate demand*. Otherwise the offer is not feasible and this is not a proper market, or these are not proper prices. Hence there arises the question of the existence of proper prices. Investigations after Walras have renewed attention to this main question in the theory of general equilibrium. It is seen now to be outstanding also for interests of Aristotle, even though these may not have been envisaged in the original motivation.

It is not enough that the existence of proper prices should be granted. There remains a question of realization, or how the system itself should discover those

---

3 This condition, familiar from the microeconomics textbooks, is 'Gossen's second law'.
4 Léon Walras, *Élements d'économie politique pure*, Lausanne, 1874.

prices, and with that discovery enter the equilibrium state where there is the universal coincidence of exchange rates to abolish Aristotle's dilemma.

The theory of general equilibrium bears also on this question. With any improper prices that may be tentatively entertained, for some good either a buyer will not find a seller, or a seller a buyer. According to 'The Law of Supply and Demand' for the movement of prices under 'market forces': in the one case, of excess demand, the price of the good would rise, and in the other of excess supply it would fall. The continuation of this tentative search or *tâtonnement*, generated from within the system by the decisions of buyers and sellers, should lead towards the equilibrium. This is the stability question investigated in the theory of general equilibrium.

Bibliography

Afriat, A. (1991). Le juste échange dans l'*Éthique á Nicomaque*. Thesis, Maîtrise in Lettres Classiques, Université Paris-IV Sorbonne.

Dempsey, Bernard W. (1935). Just price in a functional economy. *American Economic Review* 25, September.

Finley, M. I. (1970). Aristotle and economic analysis, past and present. *History of Political Economy*, May.

Gordon, B. J. (1964). Aristotle and the development of value theory. *Quarterly Journal of Economics* 77.

Gossen, H. (1854). *Entwicklung der Gesetze des menschlichen Verkehrs, und der daraus fliessenden Regeln für menschliches Handeln*, Braunschweig.

Hollander, S. (1965). On the interpretation of just price. *Kyklos* 18.

Joachim, H. H. (1951). *Aristotle. The Nicomachean ethics*. Oxford: Clarendon Press.

Ross, W. D. (1925). *The Nicomachean Ethics of Aristotle*. Oxford: Oxford University Press.

Thomson, J. A. K. (1953). *The Ethics of Aristotle*. Penguin Books.

Todd Lowry, S. (1969). Aristotle's mathematical analysis of exchange. *History of Political Economy* 1, 1 (Spring), 44–66.

Note 2

Theorems of the Market[5]

"The First and Second Theorems of Welfare Economics"

In an exchange economy where consumers have concave utility functions, the utility-possibility set is convex. This provides basis for a perhaps new approach to the well-known 'welfare' theorems.

Consider an exchange economy, with n goods and m traders. The commodity space is $C = \Omega^n$.[6] Allocations of goods to traders are given by the $n \times m$ matrices describing $D = C_m = \Omega_m^n$, so for $x \in D$,

$$x = (x_1, \ldots, x_m), \quad x_j \in C,$$

and

$$xI = \sum x_j \in C, \quad \text{where} \quad I = \begin{bmatrix} 1 \\ \vdots \\ 1 \end{bmatrix} \in \Omega^m,$$

is the aggregate of goods allocated. Then for a reallocation x of a given initial allocation $a \in D$, it is required that $xI \leq aI$.[7]

Traders have utilities $u_j : C \to \Omega$, and the utility space is $U = \Omega_m$. The mapping $u : D \to U$ determines a utility vector for any commodity allocation $x \in D$, given by

$$u(x) = (u_1(x_1), \ldots, u_m(x_m)) \in U.$$

Then the utility possibility set is

$$U(a) = \{u : u \leq u(x), xI \leq aI\}.$$

5 Econometric Society European Meeting, Uppsala, Sweden, 22–6 August 1993.
6 In present notation, with Ω as the non-negative numbers, $B = \Omega_n$ is the budget space (non-negative row vectors), and $C = \Omega^n$ is the commodity space (column vectors). Then any $p \in B, x \in C$ determine $px \in \Omega$ for the value of the commodity bundle x at the prices p.
7 For a vector v, $v \geq 0$ means $v_i \geq 0$ for all i, $v \gtrsim 0$ means $v \geq 0$ and $v \neq 0$, and $v > 0$ means $v_i > 0$ for all i.

In any case, $u(a) \in U(a)$, and also

$$v \leq u \in U(a) \Rightarrow v \in U(a).$$

If the u_j are concave, then $U(a)$ is convex.[8]

If the u_j are unsatiated in all goods, so monotonic increasing, or

$$y_j \gtrsim x_j \Rightarrow u_j(y_j) < u_j(x_j),$$

then

$$v \gtrsim u \in U(a) \Rightarrow v < u' \in U(a) \quad \text{for some } u'. \tag{i}$$

For a Pareto allocation a,

$$u \gtrsim u(a) \Rightarrow \sim u \in U(a),$$

and so

$$U(a) \cap \{u : u \geq u(a)\} = u(a). \tag{ii}$$

It is assumed first that all goods have positive aggregates, so $aI > 0$; also that $u(a) > 0$, as would follow from monotonicity if the allocation of goods to any trader is not null, or $a_j \gtrsim 0$.

THEOREM[9]

a   Equilibrium prices produce a Pareto allocation.
b   Every Pareto allocation is supported by some prices.

First consider (b). From (ii), there exists a separating hyperplane of these convex sets through their common point $u(a)$, say $u\omega = u(a)\omega$, so

$$u \in U(a) \Rightarrow u\omega \leq u(a)\omega, \tag{iii}$$

and, because of (i), with $u(a) > 0$, so that $u \gtrsim u(a)$ for all u in an open neighbourhood, it follows that

$$u \gtrsim u(a) \Rightarrow u\omega < u(a)\omega,$$

and hence that $\omega > 0$, making $u(x)\omega$ concave. According to (iii), with the definition of $U(a)$,

$$\max u(x)\omega : xI < aI$$

8 The proof is elementary. We would not have the convexity had the utility-possibility set been taken instead to be $\{u(x) : xI \leq aI\}$.
9 Commonly called 'The First and Second Theorems of Welfare Economics'.

is attained for $x = a$. With $aI > 0$, so that $xI < aI$ for some x, the Slater constraint qualification is obtained, and hence for some $p \geq 0$,

$$\max u(x)\omega - pxI$$

is attained for $x = a$.[10] But

$$u(x)\omega - pxI = \sum u_j(x_j)\omega_j - p \sum x_j = \sum (u_j(x_j)\omega_j - px_j),$$

so, with $\lambda_j = 1/\omega_j$, so that $\lambda_j > 0$, this is equivalent to

$$\max u_j(x_j) - \lambda_j px_j$$

being attained for $x_j = a_j$, for all j, which is equivalent to

$$\max u_j(x_j): px_j \leq pa_j$$

being attained for $x_j = a_j$, for all j, that is, prices p support the allocation a.

For the converse (a), it is enough that the utilities u_j be unsatiated just in some goods, or semi-increasing,

$$y_j < x_j \Rightarrow u_j(y_j) < u_j(x_j).$$

Also $pa_j > 0$ is required so that $px_j < pa_j$ for some x_j to provide the constraint qualification. Then the argument can proceed in reverse, having the $\lambda_j > 0$ and so forth with $\omega_j = 1/\lambda_j$.

Bibliography

Afriat, S. N. (1969). The output limit function in general and convex programming and theory of production. Thiry-sixth National Meeting of the Operations Research Society of America, Miami Beach, Florida, November. *Econometrica* 39 (1971), 309–39.
—— (1987). *Logic of Choice and Economic Theory*. Oxford: Clarendon Press.
Arrow, Kenneth J. (1950). An extension of the basic theorems of classical welfare economics. In J. Neyman (Ed.) Proceedings of the Second Berkeley Symposium on Mathematical Statistics and Probability. University of California Press, pp. 502–37.
—— and F. H. Hahn (1972). *General Competitive Analysis*. Edinburgh: Oliver & Boyd.
Boulding, K. (1952). Welfare Economics. In B. F. Haley (Ed.) *A Survey of Contemporary Economics*. Vol. II. Homewood, IL: Irwin.
Debreu, G. (1954). Valuation equilibrium and Pareto Optimum. Proceedings of the National Academy of Sciences of the USA, 40, 588–92.
—— (1959). *Theory of Value: An Axiomatic Analysis of Economic Equilibrium*. Cowles Foundation Monograph no. 17. New York: John Wiley.
Kreps, David M. (1990). *A Course in Microeconomic Theory*. NY: Harvester Wheatsheaf.

---

10 Principles for convex programming and the Slater constraint qualification that bear here have an account in my (1969) paper and (1987) book Part V, Chapter 1, pp. 377ff.

Lange, O. (1942). The foundations of welfare economics. *Econometrica* 10, 215–28.

Samuelson, Paul A. (1970). Maximum Principles in Analytical Economics. Nobel Memorial Lecture, Stockholm, 11 December. In *Les Prix Nobel en 1970*. Amsterdam and New York: Elsevier. Reprinted in *Science*, 10 September 1971.

Shubik, Martin (1970). A Curmudgeon's guide to microeconomics. *Journal of Economic Literature* 18, 2.

Slater, M. (1950). Lagrange multipliers revisited: a contribution to non-linear programming. *Cowles Commission Discussion Paper* Math 403 (November).

Takayama, Akira (1985). *Mathematical Economics*, 2nd edn. Cambridge: Cambridge University Press.

Varian, Hal M. (1992). *Microeconomic Analysis*, 3rd edition. NY: W.W. Norton.

Note 3

Hypothetical traders for the linear market

Source for the present topic is recollection of hearsay in the early 1970s when there was a stream of papers having to do with it, listed here in the bibliography, and then the paper of John Geanakoplos of 1984, where it is said:

> Unfortunately, many of the ideas in these important proofs are hidden by the extremely complicated nature of the constructions.

From out of respect for that importance, joined with a pursuit of simplicity, this note undertakes an examination of the topic in the framework of "The Linear Market Model" of Part III.

Market excess supply functions $S(p) \in \mathbf{R}^n$ are defined for all $p > 0$, $p \in \mathbf{R}_n$. The market as a sum of independent individuals requires the function S for the market to be a sum of functions s for the individuals,

$$S(p) = \sum s(p),$$

where, since prices are significant to the extent of determining exchange rates,

$$s(tp) = s(p) \quad (t > 0) \tag{i}$$

and since $s(p)$ represents an exchange of goods at these rates,

$$ps(p) = 0. \tag{ii}$$

Hence, by summation,

$$S(tp) = S(p) \quad (t > 0) \tag{i$'$}$$
$$pS(p) = 0 \qquad \text{(Walras' Law)} \tag{ii$'$}$$

The question considered now concerns a function S with properties (i) and (ii) joined with continuity. The question is whether such a function with just these properties can always be expressed as a sum of functions s associated with utility maximizing individuals.

For the vector $e = e(p)$ of *market value functions*

$$e_j = p_j S_j(p),$$

which give excess supplies in money or exchange value terms, it follows that

$$e(tp) = te(p) \quad (t > 0), \tag{i}''$$

$$\sum_j e_j(p) = 0. \tag{ii}''$$

Here we deal with a special case, the *linear market model*, in which the market value functions are given by

$$e_j = \sum_i p_i a_{ij}$$

for some constant a_{ij}, and so are the elements of the vector e having the linear form

$$e = pa,$$

where a is a constant matrix, the *structure matrix* for the market.

For such a model Walras' Law, generally requiring $eI = 0$ for all p, therefore, requires $paI = 0$ for all p, and hence that

$$aI = 0.^{11}$$

Accordingly, by virtue of Walras' Law, the elements in the rows of the market structure matrix all sum to 0.

For this linear market model the Slope and Intercept Conditions, dealt with in Part II Sections 2 and 3, become equivalent to each other, each being equivalent to the condition

$$a_{ij} < 0 \quad (i \neq j)$$

on the structure matrix a. A *proper linear market* is one having this condition. An equivalent condition is that

$$b = I - a$$

such that

$$b \geq 0, \quad bI = I,$$

that is, b is a row-distribution matrix, the elements in any row being non-negative with sum 1.

---

11 As before in Part II, Appendix III, I denotes a column vector with elements all 1.

Consider n traders and n goods in a 1–1 correspondence such that any trader wants a maximum quantity of its corresponding good and none at all of the other goods.

The traders $j = 1, \ldots, n$ have original endowments in the goods $i = 1, \ldots, n$ in positive amounts b_{ij} forming the columns b_j of an $n \times n$ matrix $b \geq 0$. By taking the unit used for any good as the total amount of it held in these endowments, we have

$$\sum_j b_{ij} = 1 \quad \text{for all } i,$$

that is,

$$bI = I,$$

showing b to be a square row-distribution matrix.

The economy so described we can here call a *model community*, with b as *endowment matrix*.[12]

It will appear that:

The excess supply functions for any proper linear market, with structure matrix a, are aggregates of the individual supply functions of a model community, with endowment matrix $b = 1 - a$.

With any prices given by a vector p, trader j has a value pb_j from its endowment. Hence, by supplying the bundle b_j of amounts of various goods held, the trader can demand the associated good that is wanted in the amount pb_j/p_j that has the same value. Hence, for the net supply of good i by trader j, we have

$$s_{ij}(p) = b_{ij} \quad (i \neq j),$$
$$s_{jj}(p) = b_{jj} - pb_j/p_j.$$

Therefore, by summation,

$$S_i(p) = \sum_j s_{ij}(p)$$
$$= \sum_j b_{ij} - pb_i/p_i$$
$$= 1 - pb_i/p_i$$

12 This can be seen as a special case of the Cobb–Douglas economy of Part III, Section 4, obtained by taking the want-matrix w to be the unit matrix.

and so

$$e_i = p_i S_i(p)$$
$$= p_i - pb_i,$$

that is,

$$e = p(1 - b) = pa,$$

and so we have

$$e = pa$$

where

$$a = 1 - b.$$

Bibliography

Debreu, Gerard (1974). Excess demand functions. *J. Math. Econ.* 1, 15–21.

Geanakoplos, John (1984). Utility functions for Debreu's 'excess demands'. *J. Math. Econ.* 13, 1–9. *Cowles Foundation Paper* No. 600, Yale University, 1985.

Mantel, R. R. (1974). On the characterization of aggregate excess demands. *J. Econ. Theory* 7, 438–53.

—— (1976). Homothetic preferences and community excess demand functions. *J. Econ. Theory* 12, 197–201.

McFadden, Daniel, Andrau Mas-Collel, R. R. Mantel and Marcel Richter (1974). A characterization of community excess demand functions. *J. Econ. Theory* 9, 361–74.

Sonnenschein, Hugo (1973). Do Walras identity and continuity characterize the class of community excess demand functions? *J. Econ. Theory* 6, 345–54.

Note 4

Historical note on "Data Envelope Analysis"

frontier and stochastic-frontier production functions

In giving an account of the frontier production function to an economics graduate student class in 1969 at UNC Chapel Hill, when dealing with the case where there is imposition of constant-returns, Charles Geiss, a member of the class, declared that obtaining production efficiences by such means seemed another way of representing the method proposed by M. J. Farrell (1957). That was confirmed, and Geiss, in the (1971) report, recomputed and extended Farrell's results, using the same data. He developed computer programs for carrying out test of various production models, defined by restrictive properties, and the corresponding efficiency determinations.

A constant returns function is determined by a single isoquant, and Farrell dealt with the unit isoquant instead of the function graph. However, when dealing with the function graph, instead of taking the monotone convex conical closure – a kind of "envelope" – of the data points, to get an equivalent of Farrell, one can just as well drop the conical, or constant-returns, imposition, to get something different from Farrell, with which we had started, these procedures being among those proposed by Afriat (1971). So with reference to Farrell, Afriat and Geiss we have the early history of the frontier production function, which comprises the main ideas of what is now called 'data envelope analysis'.

The stochastic-frontier production function is something else, the idea proposed originally by Afriat (1971), and computations with data first carried out by Richmond (1974).

Though we were colleagues during 1953–6 at the Department of Applied Economics, Cambridge, when I was working in association with Richard Stone on demand analysis and index numbers, I never had any encounter with Farrell to do with production efficiency. My entry into the subject came from work in demand analysis. The revealed preference consistency condition of Houthakker (1950) applied to finite demand data

$$(p_r, x_r) \in B \times C \quad (r = 1, \ldots, m)$$

with

$$M_r = p_r x_r, \quad u_r = M_r^{-1} p_r, \quad D_{rs} = u_r x_s - 1,$$

$$D_{rij\ldots ks} = (D_{ri}, D_{ij}, \ldots, D_{ks}),$$

which can be stated as denial of the possibility

$$D_{r\ldots r} \lesssim 0,$$

is equivalent[13] to the consistency of the system of homogeneous linear inequalities[14]

$$\lambda_r > 0, \quad \lambda_r D_{rs} \geq \varphi_s - \varphi_r \qquad (r, s = 1, \ldots, m).$$

If (λ_r, φ_r) $(r = 1, \ldots, m)$ is any solution then utility functions

$$\check{\varphi}, \hat{\varphi} : C \to \Omega$$

that fit the data are the polytope and polyhedral functions given by

$$\check{\varphi}(x) = \max \left\{ \sum_r \varphi_r t_r : \sum_r x_r t_r \leq x, \sum_r t_r = 1, t_r \geq 0 \right\}.$$

and

$$\hat{\varphi}(x) = \min\{\varphi_r(x): r = 1, \ldots, m\}$$

where

$$\varphi_r(x) = \varphi_r + g_r(x - x_r), \quad g_r = \lambda_r u_r.$$

Both are classical utility functions, monotonic concave, with value φ_r and gradient g_r at $x = x_r$, and if φ is any other then

$$\check{\varphi}(x) \leq \varphi(x) \leq \hat{\varphi}(x) \quad \text{for all } x.$$

The function $\check{\varphi}$ which appears here as a lower bound or "envelope" function is the one transported from demand to production analysis to make the frontier production function, with the characteristic linear programming formula, involving the given data directly. Use of such functions has given rise to what is called "the non-parametric approach", as dealt with by Varian (1982 and 1984).

Representative items from early history are in the bibliography, and for more recent ones I am indebted to Luigi Luini, and to Pierpaolo Pierani and Pier Luigi Rizzi (1999).

---

13 This is the "Afriat's Theorem" of microeconomic textbooks, Varian (1993) and Kreps (1993).
14 My 1960 paper on "The system of inequalities $a_{rs} > X_s - X_r$" is relevant to this system, as explained in a footnote there. This, following the 1956 report and this footnote, is as far as publication went prior to the 1964 paper (usually cited as of 1967). A further account is in my 1987 book.

Bibliography

Afriat, S. N. (1956). The consistency condition and other concepts in the theory of value and demand (mimeo.). Department of Applied Economics, Cambridge.

—— (1960). The system of inequalities $a_{rs} > X_s - X_r$. *Research Memorandum* No. 18 (October), Econometric Research Program, Princeton University. *Proc. Cambridge Phil. Soc.* 9 (1963), 125–33.

—— (1964). The construction of utility functions from expenditure data. *Cowles Foundation Discussion Paper* No. 144 (October 1964), Yale University. First World Congress of the Econometric Society, Rome, September 1965. *International Economic Review* 8, 1 (1967), 67–77.

—— (1968). The construction of cost-efficiencies and approximate utility functions from inconsistent expenditure data. Winter Meeting of the Econometric Society, Washington DC, December.

—— (1971). Efficiency estimation of production functions. Boulder Meeting of the Econometric Society, September 1971. *International Economic Review* 13, 3 (October 1972), 568–98.

—— (1972). The theory of international comparisons of real income and prices. In D. J. Daly (Ed.) *International Comparisons of Prices and Output*. Studies in Income and Wealth No. 37, Proceedings of the Conference at York University, Toronto, 1970. New York: National Bureau of Economic Research, pp. 13–84.

—— (1987). *Logic of Choice and Economic Theory*. Oxford: Clarendon Press.

—— (1988). Efficiency in production and consumption. In Ali Doğramacı and Rolf Färe (Eds). *Applications of Modern Production Theory: Efficiency and Productivity*. Boston: Kluwer-Nijhoff.

Aigner, D. J. and S. F. Chu (1968). On estimating the industry production function. *American Economic Review* 58, 4, 826–39.

—— and P. Schmidt (Eds.) (1980). Specification and estimation of frontier production functions, profit and cost functions. *Journal of Econometrics* (supplementary issue) 13, 1–138.

Battese, G. E. (1992). Frontier production functions and technical efficiency: a survey of empirical applications in agricultural economics. *Agricultural Economics* 7, 185–208.

—— and S. S. Broca (1997). Functional forms and stochastic frontier production functions and models for technical efficiency effects: a comparative study for wheat farmers in Parkistan. *Journal of Productivity Analysis* 8, 395–414.

—— and T. J. Coelli (1988). Prediction of firm-level technical efficiencies with a generalized frontier production function and panel data. *Journal of Econometrics* 38, 387–99.

Bravo-Ureta, B. E. (1986). Technical efficiency measures for dairy farms based on a probabilistic frontier function model. *Canadian Journal of Agricultural Economics* 34, 399–415.

—— and L. Rieger (1991). Dairy farm efficiency measurement using stochastic frontiers and neoclassical duality. *American Journal of Agricultural Economics* 73, 2, 421–8.

Charnes, A., W. W. Cooper and E. Rhodes (1978). Measuring the efficiency of decision making units. *European Journal of Operations Research* 5, 2, 429–44.

Cornwall, C., P. Schmidt and R. C. Sikles (1990). Production frontiers with cross-sectional and time-series variation in efficiency levels. *Journal of Econometrics* 46, 185–200.

Doğramacı, Ali and Rolf Färe (Eds) (1988). *Applications of Modern Production Theory: Efficiency and Productivity*. Boston: Kluwer.

Färe, Rolf, Shawna Grosskopf and C. A. Knox Lovell (1994). *Production Frontiers*. Cambridge: Cambridge University Press.

Farrell, M. J. (1957). The measurement of economic efficiency. *Journal of Royal Statistical Society*, CXX (Part 3), 253–81.

Geiss, Charles (1971). Computations of critical efficiencies and the extension of Farrell's method in production analysis. Department of Economics, University of North Carolina at Chapel Hill, mimeograph. Presented at Summer Meeting of the Econometric Society, Boulder Colorado, September.

Hanoch, G. and M. Rothschild (1972). Testing the assumptions of production theory. *Journal of Political Economy*, 256–75.

Houthakker, H. S. (1950). Revealed preference and the utility function. *Economica* N.S. 17, 159–74.

Kreps, David (1993). *A Course in Microeconomic Theory*. Englewood Cliffs, N. J.: Prentice Hall.

Meeusen, Wim and Julien van den Broeck (1977). Efficiency estimation from Cobb–Douglas production functions with composed error. *International Economic Review* 18, 2, 435–44.

Pierani, Pierpaolo and Pier Luigi Rizzi (1999). Technology and efficiency in a panel of Italian dairy farms: a SGM restricted cost function approach. *Quaderno* 258 (July), Department of Political Economy, University of Siena.

Richmond, J. (1974). Estimating the efficiency of production. *International Economic Review* 15, 515–21.

Schmidt, P. and R. C. Sickles (1984). Production frontiers and panel data. *Journal of Business and Economic Statistics* 2, 4, 367–74.

Varian, Hal (1982). The non-parametric approach to demand analysis. *Econometrica* 50, 4, 945–73.

—— (1984). The non-parametric approach to production analysis. *Econometrica* 52, 3, 579–98.

—— (1993). *Microeconomic Analysis*, 3rd edn. New York: W. W. Norton & Co.

Index

markets (*Continued*)
  feasibility question 8; forces 16; nature
    of 8; occurrence of 3; philosophy xiv;
    presence of 109; prices 108; principle,
    vindication of 61; structure matrix 27;
    system, devotees of 82; teaching 47;
    theorems of 111–13; theory of 38; and
    trade 62; value functions 12;
    values 58
Markov processes 29, 34, 38;
  theory 12, 36; transition matrix 41
Marxism 78
Marxists 48, 69; phase 51;
  philosophy 107
Marx, K. 51
mathematical economics 58
Maximum Doctrine 64; of Perfect
  competition 48
maximum problem 63
Mazurkiewicz, S. 22
microeconomics 72
military confrontation 73
mistakes, transmission of 47, 49
model community 117
Morowitz, H. 69
Moulin, H. 91
multilateral liberalization 61
mutual interference 76

nationalities 73
national power, old forms of 79
national self-sufficiency 73; concept
  of 76; economic cost 77
neoclassical economics 48, 51
New Economic Order 61
Nobel Memorial Prize 58
notation 97, 111
Notre Dame Cathedral 82

objectivity, in fair exchange 109
open markets 73
"optimality" cases of economics 67
optimisation, multi-objective 49
Optimism 58, 65, 91, 100; idea of 46
optimum 64; of general equilibrium 66;
  with global reference 68; pursuit of 67
Ottawa 57
output maximization 94

oversatiation 97
ownership and real responsibility of
  management 77

Pangloss, Dr. 66–7, 71, 100
Pareto: allocation 112; Optimism 68;
  optimum 64, 90
Pareto, V. 69, 96
Paris 82
Pastine, I. xv
patchwork of localities 51
Peleg, B. 91
Peloponnesian War 79
people and their territory, relationship 78
Pericles 78
Philips, I. 48, 70
Physiocarats 48, 64, 68; Maximum
  Doctrine of 71
Pierani, P. 120
Pitman's Synonyms and Antonyms 89–90
Polanyi, K. 50
political theory 72
Popper, K. xiii
population 61; concerns 73;
  explosion 60; independent factor of 79
preference 64, 91; order 96
price: adjustments 38; phenomenon 4;
  theory, based on supply and
  demand 6–7
Priestley, J. 48, 70
production: efficiencies 92, 119;
  functions 119; models 119;
  possibilities 11
proper linear market 116–17
protecting borders 74
protectionism 74
proximities 76, 78

Queen's University xiii
Quesnay, F. 48, 63, 68–9
Quesnay's Economic Principle 49, 68, 100

rationality 71; definition of 67; in
  economics 90
R.C. Mills Memorial lecture 63
reducibility: of economy 35–6; issue
  of 31
regional deficiencies 76
religions 73

For Product Safety Concerns and Information please contact our
EU representative GPSR@taylorandfrancis.com Taylor & Francis
Verlag GmbH, Kaufingerstraße 24, 80331 München, Germany